Afrika Afeni Mills's book fills an important gap in the arena of diversity, equity, and inclusion. She helps us understand why White students need to build their cultural competence if we are to truly have a society that is bias-free. If you're a White educator or parent, this book will help you to let go of the things that no longer serve you and to teach your students to embrace those things that will help create welcoming environments where all feel a sense of belonging.

—Zaretta Hammond, author
*Culturally Responsive Teaching and The Brain:*
*Promoting Authentic Engagement and Rigor*

Afrika Afeni Mills expertly offers just the right blend of reflective questions for increasing racial consciousness, with numerous resources, and asks us as White educators to heal ourselves so that we might provide a more accurate racial understanding for all of our students. Doing the exercises within this book is a must-do for any educator who wants to further the work of racial justice in schools.

—Jenna Chandler-Ward
Co-Founder, Teaching While White

In this book, White teachers have an answer. The work of being pro-human is hard and in some ways requires that teachers reinvent the wheel. Afrika Afeni Mills has done a fantastic job of laying out a process for these teachers to follow. From the prologue to the very end, there are nuggets of wisdom and powerful examples that offer concrete ideas. Considering the struggles our schools are facing and the needs White students have for ABAR learning, this is a timely and necessary book.

—Lorena Germán, author
*Textured Teaching: A Framework for*
*Culturally Sustaining Practices*

Afrika Afeni Mills's *Open Windows, Open Minds: Developing Antiracist, Pro-Human Students* is a must-read for K–16+ educators who want not only to espouse antiracism practices but also to do the deep transformative work required for this within schools and communities in a way that orients us all toward freedom and liberation.

—Anneliese Singh
Associate Provost for Diversity and Faculty Development/Chief Diversity Officer
Office of Academic Affairs & Provost, Tulane University

Afrika Afeni Mills's work is, in short, exceptional. She guides her readers through some of the most important reflections that we can undertake, often with a clever approach that places our answers in conversation with other thoughtful educators around the country. Next, she guides us through practical strategies that not only are grounded in the early chapters' reflective practices but also show us how to inspire students to start—or continue—their own journeys of rigorous reflection about their racial identities. I love how, when doing this, Mills never offers the empty generalities that we have become accustomed to in recent times. She instead embraces complexity and shows us how we can encourage our students to do the same. *Open Windows, Open Minds* is truly a must-read, in every sense of the phrase.

—**Matthew R. Kay,** teacher
Author, *Not Light but Fire: How to Lead
Meaningful Race Conversations in the Classroom*, and

Co-Author, *Answers to Your Biggest Questions
About Teaching Middle and High School ELA*

The key contribution of *Open Windows, Open Minds* is Afrika Afeni Mills's ability to carefully, transformatively step readers—and especially White teachers—through our own *knowing better* so that we can *do better* supporting students' abilities to know and do better.

—**Paul Gorski**
Founder and Lead Equity Specialist, Equity Literacy Institute

*Open Windows, Open Minds* is a powerful and instructive guide for White educators who are striving to become more effective allies, accomplices, and co-conspirators. Afrika Afeni Mills offers a progression of reflection and action that will empower White educators to dismantle our internalized biases and prejudices and provide better learning opportunities for our students.

—**Donalyn Miller,** teacher
Author, *The Book Whisperer*

*Open Windows, Open Minds* isn't simply a book you will read. It's a brilliant book you will reread, mark up, keep near, talk about, and encourage others to read. It's a critical text for anyone committed to living an antiracist life. It's a book you will start reading for just ten minutes and then discover you have sat still with thoughts racing for an hour. It's a how-to book that is also a why-you-must book.

—**Kylene Beers,** author
*When Kids Can't Read; Notice and Note; and Forged by Reading*
Past President of the National Council of Teachers of English

# Open Windows, Open Minds

*To Noah, Mateo, Jack H., Liam K., Fiona, Mira, Gabe, Grace, Hayden, Kellan, Camryn, Riley, Liam C., Wayne, Moira, Abraham, Lazarus, Augustine, Llewyn, Juliet, Micah, and Tyler.*

*May the words in this book help this world to become the world you deserve.*

# Open Windows, Open Minds

## Developing Antiracist, Pro-Human Students

Afrika Afeni Mills

Foreword by Cornelius Minor and Kass Minor

FOR INFORMATION:

Corwin
A SAGE Company
2455 Teller Road
Thousand Oaks, California 91320
(800) 233-9936
www.corwin.com

SAGE Publications Ltd.
1 Oliver's Yard
55 City Road
London EC1Y 1SP
United Kingdom

SAGE Publications India Pvt. Ltd.
B 1/I 1 Mohan Cooperative Industrial Area
Mathura Road, New Delhi 110 044
India

SAGE Publications Asia-Pacific Pte. Ltd.
18 Cross Street #10-10/11/12
China Square Central
Singapore 048423

President:  Mike Soules
Vice President and
  Editorial Director:  Monica Eckman
Executive Editor:  Tori Mello Bachman
Content Development Editor:  Sharon Wu
Editorial Assistant:  Nancy Chung
Project Editor:  Amy Schroller
Copy Editor:  Megan Markanich
Typesetter:  C&M Digitals (P) Ltd.
Proofreader:  Lawrence W. Baker
Indexer:  Integra
Cover Designer:  Scott Van Atta
Marketing Manager:  Margaret O'Connor

Printed in Canada

*Library of Congress Cataloging-in-Publication Data*

Names: Mills, Afrika Afeni, author.

Title: Open windows, open minds : developing antiracist, pro-human students / Afrika Afeni Mills.

Description: Thousand Oaks, California : Corwin, [2023] | Series: Corwin literacy; Volume 1 | Includes bibliographical references and index.

Identifiers: LCCN 2022015472 | ISBN 9781071852897 (paperback) | ISBN 9781071887011 (epub) | ISBN 9781071887028 (epub) | ISBN 9781071887035 (pdf)

Subjects: LCSH: Multicultural education. | Effective teaching. | Anti-racism—Study and teaching. | White people—Race identity. | Educational equalization.

Classification: LCC LC1099 .M55 2023 | DDC 370.117—dc23/eng/20220511
LC record available at https://lccn.loc.gov/2022015472

This book is printed on acid-free paper.

22 23 24 25 26 10 9 8 7 6 5 4 3 2 1

## On Children

by Kahlil Gibran (n.d.)

Your children are not your children.

They are the sons and daughters of Life's longing for itself.

They come through you but not from you,

And though they are with you yet they belong not to you.

You may give them your love but not your thoughts,

For they have their own thoughts.

You may house their bodies but not their souls,

For their souls dwell in the house of tomorrow,

Which you cannot visit, not even in your dreams.

You may strive to be like them,

But seek not to make them like you.

For life goes not backward nor tarries with yesterday.

"The paradox of education is precisely this, that as one begins to become conscious one begins to examine the society in which he is being educated."

—James Baldwin ([1963] n.d.), "A Talk to Teachers"

"If you are neutral in situations of injustice, you have chosen the side of the oppressor. If an elephant has its foot on the tail of a mouse and you say that you are neutral, the mouse will not appreciate your neutrality."

—Bishop Desmond Tutu (1984)

"Nobody's free until everybody's free."

—Fannie Lou Hamer (Ladd 2011)

"If you have come here to help me, you are wasting your time. But if you have come because your liberation is bound up with mine, then let us work together."

—Aboriginal Rights Group, Queensland, Australia, including Lilla Watson (n.d.)

# Contents

For access to antibias, antiracist (ABAR) resources,
visit the companion website for *Open Windows, Open Minds* at
**resources.corwin.com/openwindows.**

# A Foreword in Two Voices

Cornelius Minor and Kass Minor

## CORNELIUS

When I was in 6th grade, I had a White friend, and my father would never let me stay at his house for extended periods of time. Every time that I asked, the answer was, "No."

At first, the "Nos" were simple and direct. When my father could tell that I would not relent, the "Nos" became patient, yet terminal. Stop asking, Cornelius.

So when I kept pressing for weeks, the "Nos" became tense. As if to communicate, "Don't make me have to have a 'conversation' with you right here, young man."

I was 11. The last thing I wanted was a right-here "conversation" with my unyielding father. So I stopped asking.

But this was still peculiar to me, because my parents cultivated the kind of community where we shared everything—time, food, wisdom, hand-me-downs, experiences. Our living room was a meeting place, cafe, guest room, lounge, and healing center. For everyone.

My father curated a lifestyle for our family that fortified relationships by encouraging conversation, prioritizing honesty, and teaching humanity.

So being unable to spend time with Robert and his family was a mystery. Especially because Robert spent so much time with my family. So one day I asked my dad. Outright.

At the time, wisdom and strategy were nascent concepts to me, so I thought it would go really well if I asked him IN FRONT OF ROBERT.

"Hey, Daddy, why can't I ever spend time at Robert's house?"

*Stern Liberian father look*

Seconds, all of a sudden, felt like millenia.

*Stern Liberian father look pans from Robert to me*

My father exhaled in the way that Black daddies do when you MUST listen to what they are about to say next. Even Robert seemed to know that he had to pay close attention.

"Son. And . . . Robert. I am afraid. This is why you cannot visit Robert's home. Robert's parents are great friends to us, but I am afraid that Robert's parents do not know America well enough to keep you safe in it."

Each word was heavy. I remember hearing their weight then. I can feel the heaviness as I type them now.

"Cornelius, Robert's parents do not carry the same kind of worry for Robert that we are forced to carry for you in this country."

I heard what my father was telling me. I did not know then what he was teaching me. But he continued with words that echo across my consciousness still—as I parent his grandchildren.

"I've never seen Robert's parents seriously consider the history of racism in this country, and I have no way of knowing if they even understand how it impacts you every day, son. I value their friendship, but without that understanding, I cannot trust them to keep you safe in my absence."

These words are tattooed onto my consciousness.

They inform every decision that I make as a parent and as an educator. Who can keep my children, Black children, our children intellectually, emotionally, and bodily safe in my absence?

I wish that I could say, "Every teacher." In this profession, it bothers me that I cannot . . .

## KASS

In the first conversation Afrika Afeni Mills and I shared, it didn't take long for us to note the mutual joy and necessity we find within the work of building social justice in schools. While sharing the stories of our lived realities, we learned there are many roles that guide our work as both mothers and daughters, teachers and partners. We understood that for each of us, our work towards justice isn't something we just do, rather, it's who we are. We have been called upon, both spiritually and without negotiation, from the people we love the most to the people who have hurt us the worst, to make the footprint of our presence powerful.

In that first meeting (counter to the color-blind norm in the United States), we did not skip over the significance of my Whiteness and Afrika's Blackness in terms of how we navigate our work in schools as professionals: as one of the White people who makes up nearly 80 percent of the US teaching force (National Center for Education Statistics), I rarely experience a second glance when I am signing in to a school at the front desk, I have never been mistaken for anybody other than a mother or a teacher at a school. The same is not true for Afrika.

We also talked about how our racial identities impact how we are able to live our lives and mother our children. As a mother of two Black-Biracial children, already, I have witnessed my children carrying the labor of their lone racial awareness amongst most of their elementary school classmates. For most BIPOC children going to schools that are predominantly White, this is true. This, as mothers of BIPOC youth, Afrika and I share.

But being in close proximity to BIPOC people, whether they are your partner or friend or child, is not enough.

If you are White, I ask you to consider these questions through your White identity: Have you ever thought much about your race and/or racial identity? Your ancestors? Their role in the making of America? The effect of your visual appearance, the timber of your voice in the space of a classroom? Or still how much you know or don't know about the role of Black, Indigenous, and other Persons of Color (BIPOC) in your community? In history? In your personal life?

I didn't always ask those questions. In elementary school, I skirted the surface on a few of those ideas, but they were mostly banal, surface-level wonderings around physical appearance and social life. For example, I thought about the difference in hair between me and my Korean-American, Black, and Latinx friends, but I never assumed that one type of hair was more accepted by society than the other. I also wondered about the different ways our families convened during our parents' work cookouts, but I never assumed that people congregated in racial groups for a reason. Back then, I didn't unpack any power dynamics I may have noticed because no adult spoke to me about them, nor did I hear them talking about power dynamics regarding racial identity, ever. For me, the '90s were underscored with colorblindness.

As I read *Open Windows, Open Minds*, the depth of Afrika's experience, knowledge-base, and grace within her pedagogy was illuminated, and I believe her work has the power to heal, and perhaps more importantly, prevent the future harm of silence and curricular omission regarding race, identity, and social justice in schools.

For many school communities, social justice is seen as ominous, nebulous, and/or impossible. This book that Afrika has crafted is the antidote for that pushback and those notes of impossibility. Afrika brings the necessary elements for the contents of her book to come to life, providing clarity for how she enacts that love in the everyday-ness of schools with school leaders, teachers, kids, and their families. Her clarity comes in the form of powerful research, collected anecdotes from teachers and social justice agents in the field, protocols for discourse, lesson plans, as well as curriculum design frameworks.

I am the only White member of my immediate family. As I look upon my time line of "unknowing," it is with great pride and with great thoughtfulness that my own children are far more knowledgeable than I was at their age; they are capable of naming their identity markers in expansive ways, their histories are surfaced honestly, boldly, with both pride and earnest regard. From Liberia to Ireland to the United States, there is no doubt they know where they are from. My Whiteness, elements of their proximity to Whiteness, is named—not with shame, but with responsibility.

With Afrika Afeni Mills's work, White children can also have this profound experience of knowing who they are, where they come from—their honest and complicated histories. There needn't be shame, but there needs to be acknowledgement, and later, responsibility met with action.

## CORNELIUS

. . . when Robert went home that evening, my father let me stay up late, and the two of us talked for hours. He told me, "You and Robert will grow old together, and even though you love him, he will inherit his parents' silence. One day, what Robert does not know about his own Whiteness will hurt you."

This bothered me. It bothered Robert too. As we matured together, we talked about this. Frequently. When we graduated, Robert thanked my dad. He told my father, "You were right. The things that I learned in your living room were things that my parents and teachers never talked about. Even when I asked them. I am so much more prepared for the world than I would have been."

My dad's response was uncharacteristically simple. He told Robert, "There is no better feeling for a parent than knowing that the young people in the community feel prepared to meet the world."

I imagine that there is no higher praise for an educator. Afrika Afeni Mills's work leaves all of us so much more prepared for the world.

# Acknowledgments

Triune God—Father, Son, and Spirit—I have been forever changed by Your love for me, and by the unforced rhythms of Your grace, mercy, and the beauty of Your holiness. I offer You my mind and my hands. May Your gifts flow through me so that this book will help Your image bearers to experience the same uninterrupted belonging and healing that I find in You as we navigate this time of both now and not yet. Truly You taught us to love one another. Your law is love, and Your gospel is peace. May all chains be broken, and all oppression cease. Micah 6:8

Dishon, my best beloved, soul mate, and biggest cheerleader on earth. Thank you so much for supporting and believing in me. I love you with my whole heart.

Serena, Baby Girl and Queen, and Cairo, Baby Boy and my Sonshine, I love you both so much and I am so proud of who you both are. My world is so much more beautiful because you're both in it.

Rabbit, whose snuggles and love are a constant source of joy and comfort for me.

Ronald and Sandra, my parents and first teachers, your love, encouragement, and prayers have been precious gifts to me. You gave me both roots and wings, and I am deeply grateful! I love you both, and may all you invested in me return to you a hundredfold.

Gabrielle, my scoop! You are the little sister I always wanted, but I never could have dreamed of someone as special as you. May God lavish all of His richest blessings on you!

Bootsie, Dee Dee, and Ronnette, my sisters, you were all taken from this world before we really got to enjoy life with one another. But in my mind and in my dreams, we get to play together, jet skiing, laughing big belly laughs, and basking in the sun. I pray that you're all proud of me!

To unknown ancestors whose dreams I have become, am now, and am becoming, I am so grateful to you. And to those who chose the sea during the Middle Passage, I, too, choose to be unshackled by bondage and unbound by fear.

Tori Mello Bachman, doula for my words and ideas, you are not only my editor . . . you are my friend, and I am so grateful that you are in my life as a writer, yes, but mostly as a person.

Michelle (Mischa), my bosom friend and kindred spirit, with whom I am so grateful to enjoy our own raspberry cordials alongside our own lake of shining waters. The space you and I share is sacred to me.

Charlotte, everyone needs a friend with whom to enjoy magic. You are that friend to me. With you I enjoy the Shire and Rivendell, Hogwarts and Twilight. I love having a space in this world where I can be authentically myself—where there is no such thing as TMI.

Romain Bertrand, my friend and original partner in BetterLesson's Culturally Responsive Teaching and Learning work with the original coaching team. Je t'aime, mon frère, et je l'apprécie.

Jeff Broadnax, my brother who cared for me when I began to venture outside of New York City. In Orr, Minnesota, in Big Sandy, Texas, who cared for our children when they first went to overnight camp at New Heights, and whose love surrounds my family to this day.

Monica, my Ace, sister, and forever facilitation partner, I appreciate your friendship so much, and I pray that your life is continually blessed with every good thing. I will always be grateful for the doors you opened for me to participate in the National Teacher Leadership Conference, to be embraced by the National Network of State Teachers of the Year (NNSTOY) family, and to be part of your life. What an honor!

Laura, my soul sister, I love how the roots of our friendship journey during our time in Vermont have stretched, grown, strengthened, ventured beyond the soil, and established something so beautiful! It continues to bless my life with shade and fruit and contentment. I love you so, and hearing your laughter is everything!

Jenna Madeline, thank you for your constant support, love, guidance, and for always holding space for me. Walking along the beach with you, learning how to find sea glass will always be one of my fondest memories. And do we know, yet, what it means to fold in the cheese? ;)

Uche, you are one of the most beautiful, joyful sources of love in all the world. I so enjoy you—your radiant smile, exquisite voice—and how you laugh with your whole body is priceless.

Meaghan, you are absolutely one of my most favorite people in this world. Voxing with you and spending time with you is a gift to me.

Kim, you are one of the most special people I have ever been blessed to call a friend. Getting to witness the gestation, birth, and growth of *The Artful Alphabet* inspired me and helped me to see what's possible. Everything we can imagine is real, right? Our breakfast dates were life-giving to me, and I have not forgotten about our trip to DC. Let's make it happen!

Ruth, when we enrolled Serena in gymnastics as a little girl, I never imagined that from that experience I would be blessed with a friendship that developed as we watched our little girls tumble and soar. Precious serendipity! I have so much admiration and respect for you, and we will always have Amber Road.

## GRATITUDE TO THE FOLLOWING PEOPLE

Jenna Chandler-Ward and Elizabeth Denevi, who made space for my spoken words on the *Teaching While White* podcast and for my written words in the *Teaching While White* blog.

To those who made space for my voice on their podcasts, including Lindsay Lyons on *Time for Teachership*, Jen Cort on *Third Space*, Danny Bauer on the *Better Leaders, Better Schools* and *School Leadership Series*, Sheldon Eakins on *Leading Equity*, and Amplify Education on the *Science of Reading*.

Corey Scholes, who made and continues to make space every year for me and Monica at the Amplify Conference for Educators of Color.

Alex Grodd and Erin Osborn, who made space for me to develop my culturally responsive, diverse, equitable, inclusive, antibias, antiracist (ABAR) voice.

Chloe Davis-Carden for putting skin in the game with me and showing me what it looks like to discover and walk in your truth.

Sharif El-Mekki, Chris Emdin, Zaretta Hammond, and Dena Simmons, whose work continues to push and inspire me.

Winston and Laina Cox, whose love for one another, and for our children, is constant and compelling.

Loresha and Amira, my former students who not only made my time at the Tobin K–8 School beautifully memorable but who still bless my life to this day.

Education Post, for making space for my words when I first started to blog.

Debby Irving, who helped me to connect with many of the educators featured in this book.

Karen Sekiguchi, who helped me to name my firstborn book baby.

Anneliese Singh, whose words supported me through racial healing.

JoAnne Kazis and Johnny Cole, my Initiatives for Developing Equity and Achievement for Students (IDEAS) instructors.

Carly Riley, who I met at the National Anti-Racism Teach-In and who made space for me in Embracing Equity as a participant and as a facilitator.

Abby Machson-Carter, who I met at a (then) Teaching Tolerance workshop and who opened a door for me to work with MIT's Teaching Systems Lab on the Building a More Equitable Educator: Mindsets and Practices course.

Eddie Moore, who made space for me at the White Privilege Symposia, on The Privilege Institute's "Coffee with the Founder" episode, and the 2022 White Privilege Conference.

Jack Hill, who made space for my voice at the National Anti-Racism Teach-In in 2019 and 2020.

Yocelin Gonzalez, who made space for my voice at the Multicultural Teaching Institute in 2021 and 2022.

Boston Public Schools' Race, Culture, Identity, and Achievement series, Ulana and Zoe of the Boston Educators for Equity, METCO annual conferences, Ron Walker and the Coalition of Schools Educating Boys of Color Annual Gatherings, the Kauffman Foundation's Amplify: Empowering KC's Educators of Color for Student Success, Learning for Justice (formerly Teaching Tolerance) workshops, Facing History & Ourselves workshops, L'Merchie Frazier of the summer institutes sponsored and co-led by the Museum of African American History, Suffolk University, and Boston Public Schools focusing on Blacks in Boston and the abolitionist movement.

I owe a debt of gratitude to the teachers in my educational experiences who showed me what it means to create and sustain the types of learning environments that children deserve: Ms. Jamila, Ms. Kamler, Ms. Miller, Mr. Habib (the quintessential warm demander who transitioned in November 2021 as I was writing this book—may his memory be for a blessing), Mr. McDermott, Mr. Visco, and Mr. Maffei.

I owe the same to the administrators and supervisors in my teaching and coaching experiences who saw something special in me and provided opportunities for me to develop into the educator I was, am, and am becoming: Bunny Meyer, Nanzetta Merriman, Ann Deveney, and Cheryl Watson-Harris.

To my colleagues throughout my career as an educator who made work feel like family and took good care of me: Belinda Mpagazehe, Phyllis Starr, Michelle Hall, Lesley Ryan-Miller, Chandra Joseph-Lacet, Roberta Reingold, Taisha Sturdivant, and Okello Carter.

To my writing teachers and mentors who helped me to refine and develop my writing voice: Susanna Kaysen and Sandra Byrd.

I am exceedingly grateful to the educators and activists who offered their personal accounts of racial reckoning and ABAR classroom solutions to this book. You can read their words in chapters throughout the book as well as in the online companion: resources.corwin.com/openwindows:

Darcy Annino, Liz Caffey, Sydney Chaffee, Melissa Collins, Shawna Coppola, Jen Cort, Michelle Cottrell-Williams, Michael Dunlea, Leigh Ann Erickson, Jill Ferraresso, Paul C. Gorski, Nicole Greene, Sarah Halter Hahesy, Shannon Hardy, Jennifer Harvey, Marianne Hunkin, Debby Irving, Alexis Johnson, Kate LaBelle, Tiffany Lane, Kelly Lawlor, Lina Lopez-Ryan, Lindsay Lyons, Megan Mathes, Claire Miller, Sara Nadeau, Chris Odam, Amy Perrault, Shannon Pitcher-Boyea, Melissa Pointer, Kara Pranikoff, Carly Riley, Martha Santa Maria, Matt Scialdone, Eileen Sears, Karen Skeguichi, Rebecca Smoler, Shelly Tochluk, Bret Turner, Monica Washington, Jennifer Burgess Wolfrum, Brianna Young, and Kerry Zagarella.

## PUBLISHER'S ACKNOWLEDGMENTS

Corwin gratefully acknowledges the contributions of the following reviewers:

Melanie Meehan
Author and Writing/Social Studies Coordinator
Simsbury, CT

Paula Bourque
Author and Literacy Coach
Gardiner, ME

Matthew Johnson
Author and ELA Teacher
Ann Arbor, MI

Lynn Angus Ramos
Curriculum & Instruction Coordinator
Decatur, GA

# Indigenous Land Acknowledgments

I began writing this book on the unceded, stolen ancestral lands of the Massa-adchu-es-et people, in a town currently known as Randolph, Massachusetts. I finished writing this book on the unceded, stolen ancestral lands of the Catawba Nation, including the Sugaree Tribe in a city currently known as Charlotte, North Carolina.

I express my gratitude for the privilege of living on this land, as well as my broken-ness for the way that I came to live on this land and what happened to the people who first occupied and stewarded this land. May their memories be for a blessing, and may I honor their stewardship, sacrifice, and loss with the courage to speak truth and to continue learning and contributing to a reimagined world where we destroy walls and build a new table where everyone can be. Be safe, whole, truthful, humble, vulnerable, generous, brave, and filled with joy.

## FOR THE READER

I live/work in _____ (city, state),

which is the original land of the _____

_____ people.

Go to https://native-land.ca to determine the original caretakers of the land you live/work on.

# About the Author

**Afrika Afeni Mills** (she/her) is a veteran educator and an education consultant. She works with colleagues, teachers, coaches, and administrators to transform instructional practices. Afrika is regularly featured on podcasts, blogs, and webinars. Afrika also delivers keynote addresses and facilitates sessions at conferences and in schools, both virtually and in person across the United States. Afrika believes that all educators can be motivated, engaged, dynamic practitioners and leaders when provided with the support needed to create student-centered, culturally responsive learning environments that inspire wonder and creativity and nurture diversity, equity, inclusion, and belonging from an ABAR, pro-human mindset. You can connect with Afrika online at AfrikaAfeniMills.com.

# Prologue

I am a curious person, and I am particularly filled with wonder about things that veer outside of what we've come to consider as "normal." One of the things I enjoy most is reading about, listening to, watching, and learning about stories that center people working together in solidarity toward building awareness and liberation across racial differences—particularly Black and White people in the United States because I am a descendant of people who were enslaved in this country. In full disclosure, maybe it wasn't so much about solidarity and liberation at first. Perhaps my enjoyment came more from the rare opportunity to see people forming and sustaining friendships and partnerships across racial differences depicted in the media I consumed. There was something both curious and special to me about bearing witness to those relationships, especially in a society where those connections were more the exception than the rule.

The work of Emily Style of the National Seeking Educational Equity and Diversity (SEED) Project (Style 1988) and Rudine Sims Bishop (1990) regarding *windows and mirrors* provides us with a powerful frame for this book. "Books are sometimes windows, offering views of worlds that may be real or imagined, familiar, or strange. These windows are also sliding glass doors, and readers have only to walk through in imagination to become part of whatever world has been created or recreated by the author. When lighting conditions are just right, however, a window can also be a mirror. Literature transforms human experience and reflects it back to us, and in that reflection we can see our own lives and experiences as part of the larger human experience. Reading, then, becomes a means of self affirmation, and readers often seek their mirrors in books" (Bishop 1990). The problem is that White students tend to have far too few windows and far too many mirrors. What's more, even the mirrors White students have, like funhouse mirrors, often provide them with a distorted view of themselves in relationship with others.

My parents were my first teachers, and it was from them that I first learned about Black history, with the books of W. E. B. Du Bois, Ntozake Shange, Malcolm X, Maya Angelou, and Eldridge Cleaver on the bookshelves my father put up on the walls of our Brooklyn apartment. When I was a sophomore in high school, however, the person who taught my African American history class was a White man named Mr. McDermott. We read *Before the Mayflower* by Lerone Bennett Jr. (another book that I remembered seeing on a bookshelf in my home) as our text that year in addition to watching the *Eyes on the Prize* documentary series. Mr. McDermott was the first teacher to engage me as a student about Black history, including the fact that Black history long precedes enslavement. I didn't know the term *ally* then, but when I think back, especially as an educator, Mr. McDermott could have chosen to teach other subjects. He chose to teach African American history. And he chose to do it from a liberatory text and perspective. I wonder what compelled him to make this professional choice?

When I was in graduate school studying to become a teacher, I learned that Ezra Jack Keats, the author and illustrator of *The Snowy Day*, was a White man. What made him write this book featuring this little Black boy in 1962? I was also introduced to Ann Turner's book *Nettie's Trip South*, which tells the story of a young White girl's frightened and disgusted response to the horrors of enslavement. What compelled her to write this book?

When I became a teacher, I began to learn more about the abolitionist movement in the United States and to wonder about the White people who chose to offer safety, food, hiding places, diversion, clothing, rides to and for Black people who were escaping enslavement . . . those who lit lanterns and left out quilts to signal safe haven. I learned about those who authored newspapers like *The Liberator*, who spoke publicly about the ills of enslavement and the human violation of anyone attempting to own another person. I wondered about what inspired them to be who they were. William Lloyd Garrison said, in response to questions about his fiery approach to abolitionism, that "I have a need to be all on fire, for I have mountains of ice about me to melt" (Mayer 1998). What made him feel that way? What made him believe that he bore some responsibility to help melt the icy mountains of enslavement, cruelty, and oppression? What was it that compelled John Brown to organize the raid on Harpers Ferry? What made him and others like him persist in spite of backlash and scorn as well as potential and actual harm?

I went on to explore the Civil Rights Movement and noticed the light- and dark-skinned mugshots of the Freedom Riders, including White people like Joan Trumpauer Mulholland, Jim Zwerg, and David Fankhauser as they journeyed toward liberation together with Black people in the face of fear and loss. I don't believe that they were unafraid. I know their families must have been terrified for them and probably wondered why they would engage in this resistance despite the fact that they could have easily looked away. Maybe that was it. Maybe it wasn't really possible for them to look away. How did they develop the will to be courageous in the face of so many who did?

I have enjoyed reading historical fiction that explores the relationships of characters connecting across racial differences. One of my favorite examples is the fictitious relationship between Hetty (Handful) and Sarah Grimké in Sue Monk Kidd's *The Invention of Wings*. Handful is given to Sarah as a gift on her eleventh birthday, and as they grow, they both embrace abolitionism—Handful as a follower of Denmark Vesey as he is planning a revolt and Sarah as she connects with William Lloyd Garrison and becomes an abolitionist in her own right. These two characters have extremely different backgrounds yet find common ground in their sense of justice and humanity.

While it's important to be aware of the harmful impact of books and movies that exemplify a White savior narrative, portray stereotypes, or show inaccurate, white-washed, and/or White-centered views of the world, I appreciate books and movies about people and characters who connect authentically with one another across racial differences in a way that honors the humanity, dignity, and agency of the people involved in interracial relationships. Examples of how we can work in solidarity with one another in the pursuit of liberation are powerful.

Doesn't the journey toward liberation involve people who have been socialized to believe that they are better, more deserving, more intelligent, more entitled to advantages, privileges, and access to resources beginning to see that there's something not quite right with this narrative? Doesn't transformation begin to happen when those who have been designated as the dominant group see the fallacies in the way our society has been constructed—who look beyond racialization, stereotyping, prejudice, xenophobia, and bias and begin to see those who have been othered for who they truly are? To see that there are people in the world whose lives, histories, thoughts, experiences, cultures, and interests are dynamic, brilliant, creative, beautiful, and worthy of attention—and to realize that this reality has been hidden, distorted, misrepresented, denied, suppressed, and lied about.

If you, reader, are someone who identifies as White, something has been taken from you, from your parents, from your grandparents, and those who came before them. Not only were you most likely not taught the truth about people who are racially different from you as a K–12 student but you most likely didn't learn about the parts of your ancestry, like family names and traditions that were erased at Ellis Island and surrendered in order to be considered White. You may not have had the opportunity to learn that people who look like you were not only colonizers and oppressors but that there were others who, somehow, though surrounded by false messages about people of other races, didn't believe what they were being told and dedicated their lives to the pursuit of liberation through ABAR ways of being.

I'm writing this book to you, reader, as you are presently and also to younger you. The you who wondered and asked questions, the you who enjoyed being curious and investigating. The you at the age when your two front teeth were missing, when you loved to play and make friends without boundaries and walls. The you who was unhindered, curious, and undaunted—your questions about other people were not yet hushed and silenced out of politeness, or shame, or something else. The you who wondered why there weren't more People of Color in your neighborhood and schools. You deserved so much more than what was offered to you in schools and by society.

You deserved to learn to appreciate the beauty in difference.

You deserved to have your questions about racial difference answered.

You deserved the opportunity to become friends with people who were different from you.

You deserved to have neighbors who didn't look like you and to understand why there wasn't more racial diversity in your community.

You deserved to grow up unburdened and unencumbered by assumptions, stereotypes, and misinformation.

You deserved to learn how to stand up for those who are marginalized.

You deserved to know the truth about this country's history.

You deserved to grow up reading books written by people who are not like you.

You deserved to see accurate depictions in movies and on television shows of people who are different from you.

You deserved to grow up enjoying the song of the accents of languages and ways of communicating that differ from yours. The White children in our classrooms deserve the same. We have the opportunity to do things differently with and for current and future generations.

I have been an educator for twenty-three years, and during that time, I have enjoyed many amazing professional learning experiences. Some of my favorites are listed in the Acknowledgments of this book. All of these experiences were powerful and provided me with the opportunity to learn about things that were missing from my K–16 learning experiences and from my teacher preparation program. I had to pursue essential learnings like culturally responsive teaching and learning and ABAR instructional practices on my own. It wasn't part of what was required for me to be considered an effective educator, and there's still so much I need to learn. I can't help but wonder about the educator I could have been if the mosaic of learning experiences I've been able to create over time was part of my formal education all along. You may feel the same way.

I have envisioned this book to be an opportunity for me to gift back to you as a reader what I have learned from others over the years about the history of race, racialization, racial identity as well as what it looks like to work in solidarity with one another toward liberation. It is my sincere hope that it enriches your life and teaching practice the way my teachers, guides, mentors, and visionaries have enriched my understanding by sharing their wisdom with me.

This book is not about shame or guilt but about honesty, vulnerability, and openness to growth. It is about discovering the role we all can play in recreating our learning spaces. It's an invitation to become an active ally, accomplice, and co-conspirator. It is also an invitation back to that version of you as a child who was filled with wonder and curiosity and who was unafraid to ask questions, take risks, and make mistakes. And this is a book for White educators who teach in majority-White schools. Your students may not know many People of Color. They may receive confusing messages from media, family, friends, and school curriculum, yet they are part of the most racially diverse generation in history.

You may already have a road map as you engage in this work, but if not, this book is designed to equip you to be the cartographer you've been looking for. Others will benefit from the road map you will create with the support of this book. On this journey, you will go from being *unaware*, to *becoming aware*, to *acting on your awareness*, to *becoming more aware*. And because of this, those within your sphere of influence will have access to the opportunity to do the same.

This journey will not be easy. You will encounter resistance. Some resistance will be internal, because change is hard as it involves loss. Some will come from those around you who have allowed themselves to become comfortable with the status quo. I am a fan of *The Matrix* movie trilogy (okay, in full transparency, I *loved* the first movie. The last two installments, not so much). If you're also a fan, you'll remember that the main character, Neo, was offered an option by Morpheus: to take the blue pill and remain in ignorance of the disturbing reality around them, or take the red pill and learn the uncomfortable truth about that reality. Neo chooses the red pill, yet there's another character, Cypher, who, after also choosing the red pill, comes to regret his choice and decides that he would rather be reintegrated into the system to enjoy what he sees as the benefits of ignorance. You're reading this book, though, because like Neo, there is a splinter in your mind that tells you that something is not quite right with the world around us, that there are truths we need to uncover, things we need to unlearn, challenges to overcome, and a world to reimagine and rebuild.

Here are my main hopes for you, reader:

- To see how you were harmed during your K–16+ educational experiences

- To see that it is imperative to keep students from continuing to be harmed

- To move through the process of being unaware to becoming aware to acting on your awareness all the way through to becoming even more aware and continuing this cycle throughout your life

- To see that you're not alone in your pursuit of ABAR teaching practices. You are part of a larger, often unseen community of educators around the country who are engaging in this work. You will meet educators like Sarah, Leigh Ann, Sydney, Carly, Shannon, Michael, and Shawna in these pages.

- To examine your own racial identity and how it has been formed

- To equip you with strategies for decentering Whiteness in your literacy curriculum in order to manifest true antiracist teaching practice

- To find concrete examples of ways you can engage in ABAR instructional practices

- To be undaunted in the face of resistance

This book will help you to let go of the things that no longer serve you and to teach your students to do the same. In these pages, you will be wooed to a window you hadn't noticed before. Though the curtains are closed, light streams in at the edges, as light tends to do. In response to the call of the light's invitation, you will take hold of the fabric, pull it apart, and feel the warmth of the sun. You'll open the window, breathe in the fresh air, and smell the aroma of the unfamiliar and beautiful. You'll see things you've never seen before, and you'll invite your students to come and stand alongside you. Together you will gaze and behold, wonder and learn, and because of this, your students will begin to open windows of their own.

# Introduction

When my children were little, I bought clothes for them that I thought were cute. It started out with adorable onesies and shoes that they didn't need, because they weren't yet walking, and quickly outgrew. Sure, I bought clothes for them that were appropriate for each season (which was a bit tricky in New England), but in the fall and winter, their shirts were long-sleeve versions of the same types of short-sleeve shirts I had purchased in the spring and summer.

At times, I made these choices because of "gendered" influences and options (pinks for Serena and blues for Cairo) and at other times because they were just what I liked—or maybe what I wish I had been able to wear when I was little. Sometimes there were messages on the shirts, but they were messages I agreed with. They reflected my tastes, style, and preferred colors. There were very few times, even as they grew older and developed their own preferences, when I asked them what they wanted to wear. At one point, though, Cairo threw down the gauntlet. He refused to wear two items of clothing—striped (or what he called "stripy") shirts and jeans. It was pretty maddening for me and my husband. His refusal seemed random and unnecessary. As a parent, I liked being able to throw on a pair of jeans. To me, they provided versatility (matched with most tops) and convenience (no need to iron). But to Cairo they were stiff and constricting. They didn't offer the freedom of movement that came with athletic shorts and sweatpants. How he felt in his clothes mattered.

Clothes selection is one of the ways we stamp and constrain our children with our ways of being. We clothe them not only in the apparel of our choosing but in our opinions, ideas, and conclusions. Like ill-fitting clothes, these impositions can be restricting, like how Cairo felt in jeans, and can hinder their growth and stunt their racial, social, emotional, and psychological development. Take, for example, this picture of a toddler dressed as a member of the Ku Klux Klan (Gill 2013) standing in front of a Black state trooper in Gainesville, Georgia, in 1992 (see Figure 0.1). This child did not choose to be dressed this way and had no idea what this outfit meant. An adult in this child's life who is very aware of what it means chose to dress the child this way. As educators, let's not "clothe" our students in the same way we were when we were their age.

FIGURE 0.1   Toddler Dressed as a Member of the Ku Klux Klan

SOURCE: *The Times* (Gainesville, GA)

## THE URGENCY OF OPEN WINDOWS

This book is an invitation to educators to clothe the students in our classrooms with garments that give them space to grow, move, and breathe. Where they can be unhindered, unburdened, and free. And, with such freedom to move and breathe, children will be able to explore new perspectives about themselves and others. We educators can open windows and let that fresh air in, particularly for White-identifying students, who have yet to explore racial identity, antiracist thinking, and pro-human action. Opening windows can open minds and liberate us all from the bonds of racism.

My reasons for writing this book are somewhat selfish. The racial incidents that have taken place in the United States over the past several years have been concerning to me, and I'm sure it has been to many of you too. Consider these events that took place in schools in 2021 alone:

In April 2021, ABC News reported that three Wisconsin middle school teachers resigned from their positions after putting together an activity for their sixth-grade students asking how they would punish slaves.

In the summer of 2021, we heard story after story about the discoveries of the unmarked graves of hundreds of Indigenous children at "residential schools" in Canada.

In September 2021, it became widely publicized that the Central York School district in Pennsylvania had banned four pages of resources by and about People of Color the previous November when the list was distributed to teachers in August 2021.

In September 2021, students at a Kansas City high school circulated an online petition to "bring back slavery."

In October 2021, a second-grade teacher in Maplewood, New Jersey, was reported to have forcibly removed the hijab of one of her students. In the same month, a teacher at Ridgefield Memorial High School in Ridgefield, New Jersey, was accused of telling a Muslim student that "we don't negotiate with terrorists" when the student asked for a homework extension.

Again in October 2021, school board member Mary Beeman from Guilford, Connecticut, is reported to have stated, "Helping kids of color to feel they belong has a negative effect on White, Christian, or conservative kids."

Also in October 2021, a teacher in Riverside, California, was placed on leave after mocking Native Americans during her math class. A Native American student in her class recorded the mocking actions, as he felt that violence was being committed against him.

In each of these instances of individual or school-enforced racism—and in the countless others that go unreported across the United States—while Students of Color are overtly harmed, White students are not receiving a true education either. They're not learning to become citizens of the real world. As James Banks (2007) so eloquently states in *Educating Citizens in a Multicultural Society*, "To help students acquire reflective and clarified cultural, national, and global identifications, citizenship education must teach them *to know, to care, and to act* (italics added). As Freire [1985] points out, students must be taught to read the word and the world. In other words, they must acquire higher levels of knowledge, understand the relationship between knowledge and action, develop a commitment to act to improve the world, and acquire the skills needed to participate in civic action" (Banks 2007, 26).

The children in our schools right now are our future jurors, teachers, engineers, voters, designers, officers, parents, representatives, therapists, lawyers, doctors, musicians, actors, drivers, board members, school committee members, writers, and coaches. If we don't alter our typical ways of educating children, what are the outcomes we can expect in the future? As much as it depends on us, let us create and sustain learning communities as soil that is far less likely to nurture and grow the mindsets and actions of young men like Kyle Rittenhouse and Dylann Roof. Let us make sure that strange fruit doesn't continue to grow. At the very least, not on our watch.

## How to Use This Book

I've written this book in a way that asks you to use it instead of simply reading it because engaging in ABAR work requires actively thinking, doing, and evolving. In other words, this is not a sit-and-read book but a think-and-do book.

Chapters in Part 1 explore *why* racial identity work is crucial for White students—but first, for their teachers. In Chapter 1, we will dig in to the concepts of windows and mirrors and the problems that arise from White students having far too many mirrors and far too few windows. In the United States, many of our communities are hypersegregated, and much of what White students tend to "know" about people with other racial identities can come from stereotypes and misinformation, so just being aware of our biases is not enough. We need to address the false narratives about marginalized groups that tend to proliferate when segregation keeps us from truly knowing one another. This chapter examines what we can do about the harm our biases can cause by building on what ABAR practitioners wish they had known as White students during their K–12 educational experiences. What these practitioners have shared can serve as a foundation for exploring what's missing from the learning experiences we tend to provide for White students.

Although race is a social construct, it has significant meaning and power in our society. In order to equip White students as global citizens, teachers need to both learn about and teach students about the stages of White racial identity development as well as the impact of Whiteness, racialization, and privilege on relationships, communities, and systems. Chapter 2 includes tools to help readers engage in their own racial identity exploration so that they can effectively support students to do the same.

Teachers need to learn about racial identity development practices, just as all aspiring teachers engage in child and adolescent development study as part of teacher preparation programs. Equipped with more insights about your own racial identity, in Chapter 3 you will learn how to engage in relationship and community building necessary to help students to co-create a learning community where they can bravely explore their racial identities and develop inclusive and equitable ways of being.

Chapter 4 examines the typical challenges that educators face when it comes to implementing ABAR instructional practices and ways to navigate those challenges as well as the resistance that educators face when engaging in this work with students. This is particularly critical in the face of concentrated efforts to ban and, in some cases, penalize ABAR work.

Chapters in Part 2 show readers *how* to provide White students with more windows. Chapter 5 will support you as you provide students with regular opportunities to engage with accurate and inclusive history as well as content representing the lives, interests, contributions, experiences, and perspectives of other races of people. You will also be equipped to support students to engage in productive struggle as they challenge false narratives about people from marginalized groups and to adopt a growth mindset about their ability to continue this learning.

Chapter 6 explores the benefits of teaching students how to engage in discourse and the instructional moves to help students develop their discussion skills. In addition to helping learners to engage in meaningful research, teamwork, and develop analytical skills, learning to engage in critical discourse will also help them to understand the importance of developing compelling, rational, reasoned arguments to support purposeful discussion and dialogue and to integrate their developing knowledge of the perspectives and experiences of marginalized groups and to lay the foundation for solving societal challenges.

Chapter 7 will help you to integrate what students have learned about their own racial identity and the histories, perspectives, experiences, and lives of marginalized people to explore potential solutions to complex societal challenges. It will show how action-oriented learning can help students to develop 21st century skills like planning, critical-thinking, reasoning, communication, cross-cultural understanding, and decision-making through the design process. When students develop these skills, they can transition from remembering and understanding to applying, analyzing, evaluating, and creating by actively engaging in real-world and personally meaningful learning experiences.

I invite you to pay attention to these other pieces of this book, as they offer important checkpoints along the journey.

## BREATHE AND REFLECT

As is reflected in the title of Michelle Obama's autobiography, we are all in the process of becoming, as are our students. While we engage in this transformative work, we need to take time to reflect on what we read in these chapters and to think about the impact that it has on our lives and our instructional practices. The moments you invest in reading, pausing, and reflecting will equip you to begin to apply what you've learned, set intentions, and create the road map that will guide your way forward.

ONLINE COMPANION

In the online companion, found at resources.corwin.com/openwindows, you will find the following content:

- **Guidance to My Younger Self Letters:** There are ABAR mentors, guides, and supporters who are co-journeying with you. You'll meet some of them in the online companion to this book. White educators have written letters to their younger selves providing advice and guidance based on things they wish they had known and experiences they wish they had earlier in their lives. Letters have been contributed by educators and ABAR practitioners to help you know that you're not alone on this journey.

- **Additional Resources:** There are many resources that can assist us in our journey toward ABAR practices, including books, documentaries, podcasts, blogs, movies, and organizations. You can access those resources in the online companion to this book.

## Terms and Shared Considerations

I will use some terms in this book that you may find triggering, or I may use words differently than you have become accustomed to. I want to ensure that you understand what these phrases mean so that you can grapple with how they make you feel before you encounter them later in the book. Language is both important and fluid. These terms and considerations represent my best, present understanding of the most considerate way to use language.

**ABAR:** Antibias (actively against bias), antiracist (actively against racism)

**Abolitionist:** Someone who works actively to bring an end to any oppressive practice or institution.

**Advantage:** Having the access to resources and presupposition of ability, employability, innocence, intelligence, and worth because of the racial group you have been assigned to and/or most identify with. I use the term *privilege* in the same way.

**Allies:** People who *actively* align themselves with efforts to shine light and truth on and bring an end to unjust practices and ways of being. This differs from *performative allies* who state ABAR beliefs and intentions, but those statements are more about impression management than actual transformation.

**Antibias:** A commitment to becoming aware of and informing our biases with accurate experiences and information.

**Antiracist:** A commitment to interrupting race-based, systemic injustices and ideological, internalized, interpersonal, and institutional oppression.

**BIPOC:** Black, Indigenous, and People of Color. Please note that although intended to be inclusive, it can have the impact of erasing racial/ethnic identity. The same is true for the terms *People of Color* and *Students of Color*.

**Capital *B* and *W*:** I choose to capitalize the first letter of *Black* and *White* when describing people in those racial groups.

**Culture:** The customs, arts, social institutions, and ways of being of a particular nation, people, or other social group.

**Ethnicity:** Belonging to a social group with a common national or cultural tradition.

**Gender inclusivity:** Wherever possible and known, I have included the pronouns of the people I interviewed for this book and have tried to avoid using gendered pronouns, unless the pronouns belong to the person to whom I am referring.

**Marginalized:** When you think of a piece of paper, there is the center of the page and the margins. Historically and currently, the experiences, contributions, histories, needs,

*(Continued)*

(Continued)

wants, and perspectives of people who are not White, male, heterosexual, cisgender, able-bodied, and Christian have been pushed to the periphery.

**Pro-human:** Being committed to continually developing an awareness of the policies, practices, and systems that provide consideration, justice, opportunities, protection, recognition, rights, resources, and support for some, and working diligently to ensure that *all people* within one's sphere of influence have access to the same—everything leading to life, liberty, and the pursuit of happiness.

**Race:** A social construct with no biological meaning designed to classify groups of people. Many believe that race is a way to define physical differences between people, but it has actually been used as a tool of division and oppression.

**Racial identity:** What is externally imposed (what others perceive) and internally constructed (how one identifies themselves) related to our racial groups.

**Supremacy:** Believing and behaving as if one group of people is superior to all others in authority, power, status, and worth.

## Important Terms to Reflect On

**Accomplice:** This word has typically been affiliated with assisting someone with something illegal, though, in the context of ABAR practices, it can mean to assist in the effort to bring light to and interrupt unjust practices, policies, and ways of being. It's important to be aware, though, of the negative connotation of this term and how its use can pose a barrier, because liberatory work should not be equated with criminal behavior. The same holds true for the term *co-conspirator*. The *crime* is in the unjust policies, practices, and ways of being, not in engaging in freedom work.

**At-risk:** Though this term is typically used for Students of Color, I contend that White students who don't have access to ABAR instructional practices are at risk of harming themselves, others, and working against the democratic values the United States espouses in word, if not always in practice.

**Diverse:** This is often used as a euphemism when people are uncomfortable with naming race or other identity differences (for example, diverse candidates or students—or worse yet—diversity hires). I try not to use it for that purpose. I believe we should speak truthfully and be clear about what we mean. Our tendency to be indirect or less than honest about what we mean is a sure sign that there is work to be done.

**Minorities:** I will not refer to anyone who is a Person of Color as a minority, especially considering that People of Color are the global majority. I believe that the term *minority*, when referencing People of Color, can be used to minimize the worth instead of referring to numbers or percentages, or, more truthfully, exploring the *why* behind the numbers we see. For example, though Indigenous People in the United States currently represent 2% of the population, I can't help but wonder what that percentage would have been without genocide, without stolen land, without the spread of disease, without the Trail of Tears, without Indian "residential/boarding" schools, and continual violation of treaties. Similarly, though Black people in the United States currently represent 14.2% of the population, we will never know what that percentage would have been without the Middle Passage and enslavement, without lynchings, without mass incarceration, without forced sterilization and inequitable access to health care, without environmental injustices and fair access to housing and employment, and without the epigenetic manifestation of diseases.

**People First Language:** I believe that all people have inherent worth. To that end, I use terms like *enslaved person* versus *slave*, because slavery was an imposition, not the identity of the people whom the institution of slavery attempted to dehumanize.

# PART 1

# WHY WINDOWS ARE CRUCIAL FOR WHITE TEACHERS AND STUDENTS

# CHAPTER 1

# Windows for White Students

I was twelve when I first experienced someone calling me the N-word. Actually, it wasn't just someone. It was a car full of someones. My family didn't have the opportunity to go on many vacations, but as part of a festival celebration in a church we had just joined the year before, we traveled to St. Petersburg, Florida. I had only ever stayed in a hotel a couple of times before that, and only when traveling with other families. That week had been one of the most fun weeks of my life—the operative words being *had been*. On the last day of the festival, as we returned to our hotel after the church service, a car full of what appeared to be teenage White boys yelled "N*****s!" out of the open windows of their pickup truck as they drove by.

I can't help but wonder how different things may have been for my family and for those boys had someone taught them an honest version of the history of the United States. What if someone had taught them that race was a social construct, to resist participating in the cruelty of racial oppression, and to value diversity, equity, inclusion, belonging, justice, and an antibias, antiracist (ABAR) view of the world? What if someone had taught them that to hate and oppress people because of their skin color diminished their own humanity? What if they had learned US history in a way that decentered Whiteness as the default? I don't believe that those teenage boys were taught any of these things, and so that day in St. Petersburg, Florida, is part of my story—and similar incidents are part of the stories of far too many people who look like me. The boogeyman of racism that my parents had warned me about became very real to me that day—cold eyes reflecting images of auction blocks, burning crosses, and nooses; razor-sharp teeth and claws; bone-chilling growl and all.

The best way for us to learn to challenge stereotypes and false narratives about people who differ from us is to develop and sustain meaningful relationships with one another. Despite regular efforts to build and sustain integrated spaces in our society, however—neighborhoods, schools, places of worship, workplaces—spaces where people of all identities can thrive and learn from one another, our country is still racially segregated.

As educators, particularly those of us who are teaching in schools and districts mostly composed of White students, we have the opportunity to be active change agents. We can evaluate the content we teach and the learning experiences we design and facilitate to determine where we need to engage students with opportunities to identify biases and stereotypes, and learn from other perspectives and ways of being. These types of learning experiences lay the foundation for students becoming critical thinkers, and those who will be equipped to not only challenge and dismantle systems of oppression but reimagine and rebuild something much better, inspired by the freedom dreams that come from transformed ways of thinking and being.

## WHAT WE MEAN WHEN WE TALK ABOUT WINDOWS

Over thirty years ago, Rudine Sims Bishop wrote her seminal article "Mirrors, Windows, and Sliding Glass Doors," which discusses how children's books can be windows into the realities of others, and books can be mirrors that reflect the lives of readers. Too often in our schools, books serve as mirrors that reflect the lives of White readers. In this book I aim to help you to provide more window experiences for students—and to open those windows to help White students understand the lived experiences of people whose experiences have been marginalized by school and society for too long. Open windows lead to open minds.

As Sarah Park Dahlen (2019) and David Huyck's (illustrator) *2018 Diversity in Children's Books* infographic shows (see Figure 1.1), White children are surrounded by mirrors in children's books. It's important to note the following:

- The representation of American Indian/First Nations people increased from less than 1% in 2012 to 0.9% in 2015 to 1% in 2018.

- The representation of Latinx people increased from 1.5% in 2012 to 2.4% in 2015 to 5% in 2018.

- The representation of Asian Pacific Islander/Asian Pacific American people increased from 2% in 2012 to 3.3% in 2015 to 7% in 2018.

- The representation of African/African American people increased from 3% in 2012 to 7.6% in 2015 to 10% in 2018.

FIGURE 1.1 2018 Diversity in Children's Books

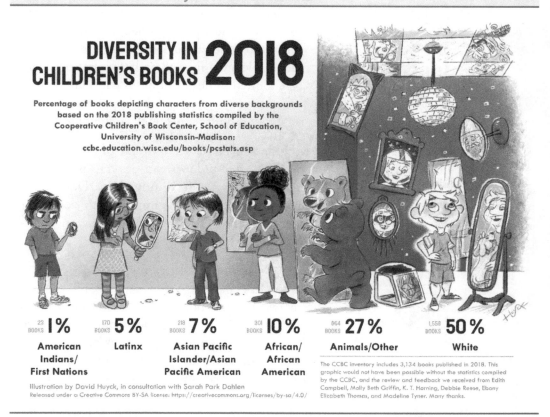

**DIVERSITY IN 2018 CHILDREN'S BOOKS**

Percentage of books depicting characters from diverse backgrounds
based on the 2018 publishing statistics compiled by the
Cooperative Children's Book Center, School of Education,
University of Wisconsin-Madison:
ccbc.education.wisc.edu/books/pcstats.asp

| 23 BOOKS **1%** | 170 BOOKS **5%** | 218 BOOKS **7%** | 301 BOOKS **10%** | 864 BOOKS **27%** | 1,558 BOOKS **50%** |
|---|---|---|---|---|---|
| **American Indians/ First Nations** | **Latinx** | **Asian Pacific Islander/Asian Pacific American** | **African/ African American** | **Animals/Other** | **White** |

The CCBC inventory includes 3,134 books published in 2018. This
graphic would not have been possible without the statistics compiled
by the CCBC, and the review and feedback we received from Edith
Campbell, Molly Beth Griffin, K. T. Horning, Debbie Reese, Ebony
Elizabeth Thomas, and Madeline Tyner. Many thanks.

Illustration by David Huyck, in consultation with Sarah Park Dahlen
Released under a Creative Commons BY-SA license: https://creativecommons.org/licenses/by-sa/4.0/

Sarah Park Dahlen (2019)

- The representation of White people decreased from 93% in 2012 to 73.3% in 2015 to 50% in 2018. As the representation of White people decreased between 2015 and 2018, there was a 14.5% increase in the percentage of animals and inanimate objects (e.g., trucks) from 12.5% to 27%, which is more of an increase than in the representation of all of the groups of Black, Indigenous, and People of Color (BIPOC) combined.

While publishers are making small steps toward diverse racial representation in children's books, we also see that there are even larger steps being taken to give the illusion of increased racial diversity while really maintaining the status quo. This overrepresentation of White people and erasure of People of Color in children's books extends to the content in K–12 classrooms, particularly in the way "classics" in English language arts and US history are taught. The International Literacy Association's *Children's Right to Read Campaign* highlights the fundamental rights that we deny children when we fail to provide access, choice, and windows and mirrors for all children and their reading lives.

https://bit.ly/3v5VpC2

We'll take a deeper dive into how to navigate resistance and opportunities to engage in interdisciplinary learning experiences that span across all content areas in later chapters. It's worth acknowledging now, though, the pressures across the United States to suppress curriculum around race/gender studies and the impact that this censorship has on students in all content areas.

When Whiteness is centered as the norm, as we see in many of our traditional curriculum and teaching practices, White students can develop uninformed, harmful mindsets. In his "Mirrors, Window, and Sliding Glass Doors" TED Talk, high school student Akhand Dugar discusses the impact of this erasure on students and the importance of shifting our literacy practices.

https://bit.ly/3vCyxcx

As a result of this lack of windows, segregation, and not engaging White students in meaningful conversations about the impact of racialization, White students can develop uninformed, harmful mindsets and ask questions or make statements that impact people from marginalized groups as microaggressions, like the following:

*When I look at you, I don't see color.*

*Why don't we have a White History Month?*

*Affirmative action is racist.*

*It's unpatriotic to kneel during the national anthem!*

According to the research of the Children's Community School (2018) in their infographic (shown in Figure 1.2), *They're Not Too Young to Talk About Race!*,

"By five, Black and Hispanic children in research settings show no preference toward their own groups compared to Whites; White children at this stage remain strongly biased in favor of whiteness" (Dunham, Baron, and Banaji 2008). It goes on to state that "silence about race reinforces racism by letting children draw their own conclusions based on what they see. Teachers and families can play a powerful role in helping children of all ages develop positive attitudes about race and diversity and skills to promote a more just future—but only if we talk about it!" As Sims Bishop states, "It's not just children who have been underrepresented and marginalized who need these (diverse) books. It's also the children who always find their mirrors in the books and therefore get an exaggerated sense of their self-worth and a false sense of what the world is like." The major goal of this book is to raise

FIGURE 1.2   They're Not Too Young to Talk About Race!

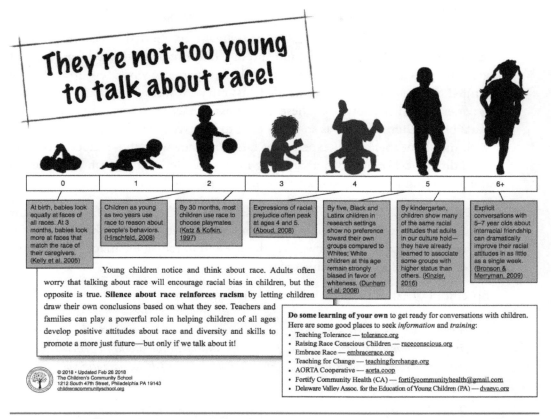

SOURCE: Infographic created by the Children's Community School, based in part on information and ideas from Jillian Addler at FirstUp, Lori Riddick at Raising Race Conscious Children, and kiran nigam at the Anti-Oppressive Resource and Training Alliance. Copyright 2018.

awareness about the harmful impact of neglecting to provide support for students as they grapple with crucial questions about race and to equip educators to push against the temptation to remain silent with our students.

## ANTIBIAS TRAINING IS NOT ENOUGH: LEARNING FROM THE TESTIMONIES OF ABAR PRACTITIONERS

In 2018, several incidents gained media attention across the United States where White people called the police on Black people for things like sitting in Starbucks, barbecuing in a park, attempting to redeem a coupon at CVS, or entering their own apartment building. Police were even called on a child who mistakenly brushed past a woman with his backpack. The response was often to provide implicit bias training. But simply being aware of our biases is not enough. In the United States, many of our communities are hypersegregated, and much of what

White students tend to "know" about people with other racial identities can come from stereotypes and misinformation. What do we do about the harm our biases can cause?

I reached out to several White colleagues who are committed to ABAR practices as educators, teacher developers, and authors. These individuals are from different generations with a variety of years of teaching experience who grew up across the United States in different regions of the country. However, they had very similar experiences, which shows that these are not experiences that are isolated to certain parts of the United States as so many tend to believe. They shared their thoughts with me about their racial experiences and how they wish those experiences had been different. I've included a sampling in this chapter, and you can find more in the online companion: resources.corwin.com/openwindows.

These accounts reaffirmed for me the need for educators to connect about the impact of our own racial socialization—and in so doing to realize that we're not as isolated in our experiences as we may think—and to reimagine much better learning experiences for our students today.

Specifically, I asked them each the following questions:

- *When do you recall first noticing racial differences between you and other people (in your community, school, place of worship, and/or in the world in general)? Did you say anything to your family about what you noticed? If so, how did your family respond to you?*

- *When was the first time you remember seeing and/or reading about people of other races in books, movies, and/or TV shows? Reflect on those books, movies, and/or TV shows.*

- *Growing up, what do you remember your K–12 teachers and/or school doing that clearly showed they didn't understand the history, culture, and oppression of People of Color?*

- *If you could go back in time with a magic wand, what changes would you make to your K–12 learning experiences related to people of other races?*

- *If you could go back in time with a magic wand, what changes would you make to your K–12 learning experiences related to being White?*

Over the following pages, I present a sampling of the responses to these questions, along with a summary of major themes that I gleaned about each question. As you read these educators' responses, please reflect on the questions yourself; there is space within the Breathe and Reflect sections of each segment for you to record your own thoughts. You will also find a Ways to Respond section after the reflections on each question. Please be sure to approach the Ways to Respond not as a checklist but as important considerations for educators.

When do you recall first noticing racial differences between you and other people (in your community, school, place of worship, and/or in the world in general)? Did you say anything to your family about what you noticed? If so, how did your family respond to you?

"I am fairly confident that I didn't notice anything—including how racially homogenous my community was—until I began school and became acquainted with a classmate of mine who was Korean and who was adopted by a White family. I didn't talk about race with my family until I was older, and they never talked about it with me, as far as I can remember. I don't recall noticing race in my surroundings unless we were at a large amusement park or something where folks from neighboring states came together for recreation."

—Shawna Coppola, educator, consultant, and author of *Renew: Become a Better and More Authentic Writing Teacher* (2017) and *Writing Redefined: Broadening Our Ideas of What It Means to Compose* (2019)

"In first grade. I don't think I had the language even of 'race' to describe the differences or talk about it. But I do remember disagreeing with [a family member] when he would say racist things, even when I was seven or eight years old."

—Paul Gorski, founder of the Equity Literacy Institute author of *Reaching and Teaching Students in Poverty* (2013) and coauthor of *Cultivating Social Justice Teachers (2013)* and *Case Studies on Diversity and Social Justice Action* (2013)

"Elementary school (starting in first grade). I didn't say anything because my first experience made it clear to me I wasn't 'supposed' to talk about this (negative encounter with my first-grade teacher who overheard a conversation I was in and concluded we were being racist so told us to 'never talk like that again,' which scared the heck out of me). I NEVER talked about it at home."

—Jennifer Harvey, college educator, director of the Crew Scholars program at Drake University (Iowa), and author of four books about disrupting White supremacy and social justice

"Kennewick was a very White, conservative town. There were very few Latinx people and even fewer Black and Asian families. I recall being about ten and hearing my grandfather speak very negatively about a biracial couple and knowing in my heart what he was saying was wrong but not having the words to describe it. I didn't feel brave enough to say anything to him at the time."

—Melissa Pointer, public school educator and elementary school principal in a school leading the implementation of instruction on race and identity

"I don't recall ever thinking about race or my own skin color until I was in a gymnastics class when I was six or seven. I was sitting next to another little girl, and we were both wearing leotards and our bare legs were next to each other. She pointed to my bare leg

*(Continued)*

(Continued)

and said, Ew, you're really pale.' In my memory, her skin looked very tan, however I do not recall her racial or ethnic identity.

"This was the first time I remember making a connection that skin color held value, and when I asked my mom about what it meant that my skin was pale, she just said that it was because I was a redhead (both my parents and my brother all have red hair and very White skin just like my own, so I always thought it was just 'normal'). Otherwise, we didn't talk about race or Whiteness in any way."

—Carly Riley, director of virtual learning and a facilitator for Embracing Equity

Reading through these responses, you notice the following themes:

- Noticing race around ages six or seven but realizing it's not something to talk about

- Receiving negative info or misinformation when asking questions about people who are not White

# Breathe and Reflect

When do you recall first noticing racial differences between you and other people (in your community, school, place of worship, and/or in the world in general)? Did you say anything to your family about what you noticed? If so, how did your family respond to you? ■

_____

_____

_____

_____

_____

_____

_____

_____

_____

_____

_____

_____

_____

_____

_____

_____

_____

_____

_____

_____

_____

_____

_____

# Ways to Respond

- If you are working in a racially segregated community where most/all of the people are White, consider what you think about how this came to be. What do your students think about it? Provide opportunities for your students to ask the race-related questions that are on their minds.

- Since White students, especially in homogenous communities where there are few or no People of Color, often struggle with seeing themselves as having a race instead of thinking of people who look like them as "normal," embed opportunities for your students to talk about their race. Make the implicit explicit.

- Provide opportunities for your students to grapple with any messages they have picked up on that they may be more intelligent than another group of people because of their race. This may cause you to take a hard look at some of our educational practices like labeling certain students as gifted and talented/advanced and academic tracking.

- Find out what your students think about Indigenous People, Columbus Day, and Thanksgiving. Are they aware of the origins of the land where your school is located? What do they know about the original caretakers of that land? Are they holding on to a deficit narrative about Indigenous People? As you're asking these questions of your students, it will be important for you to answer these questions yourself.

- Find out if your students have stereotypical beliefs about Black, Latinx/a/o, Asian and Pacific Islander, and Middle Eastern/North African (MENA) people. If they do, prepare to offer an accurate narrative.

- Consider if there are ways that the perception of being a "good White person" has hindered ABAR action in your school community. How is goodness defined?

- If there are transracial adoptees who are Students of Color in your school community, find out what their experience has been in the school and if there are any shifts you can make in your instructional practices that will improve their family's experience in your school.

- If your students are experiencing discomfort because of hearing racist comments from family and/or community members, consider how you can create space for your students to process and find words for their feelings.

When was the first time you remember seeing and/or reading about people of other races in books, movies, and/or TV shows? Reflect on those books, movies, and/or TV shows.

"I was a voracious reader as a child. I read anything I could get my hands on, and I went to the library each week and checked out the maximum number of books allowed (8). . . . I recall reading one book when I was young. In it, the author talked about a 'colored girl.' Having never heard the word *colored* used in reference to race before, my mental image of this character in the book was of a little girl with rainbow skin. The story in that book seemed magical to me as a result. I read books alone and didn't talk to anyone about them, usually, so this misinterpretation wasn't corrected by anyone. But the mental image of the little rainbow girl stuck in my head for whatever reason. Only years later, when I was much older, did I realize that the book had been referring to a Black girl. I wish that I could remember what book it was and go back to read it again now. It wasn't a magical story after all."

—Sydney Chaffee, teacher of Humanities 9 and instructional coach at Codman Academy Charter Public School, Boston, Massachusetts

"I was a child of the '90s, so I watched *Family Matters, Hangin' With Mr. Cooper, A Different World, The Cosby Show,* all the stuff on mainstream TV. This always felt normal to me. Again, no one really talked to me about race, and likely the times this topic was addressed in these shows, it went over my head. As far as books go, the first book I read by a Black writer was in eleventh grade, and only because we had an independent author study, and I chose Alice Walker. I remember being so drawn to *The Color Purple* that I started reading other Black female authors on my own—Maya Angelou, Toni Morrison, and Zora Neale Hurston, I remember. Again, I feel like I had no clear racial consciousness, but I do remember being drawn to those stories. In school, I never read a whole class novel by a BIPOC as far as I can remember."

—Leigh Ann Erickson, founder of Undone Consulting and Undone Movement; author of the young adult book *What Is White Privilege?*; educator and developer of the Connect, Absorb, Respond, and Empower (CARE) curriculum and conference

"I know I had the Babar book series. I never thought of them as racist or including POC until later in life when a page was pointed out to me. On that page are 'African cannibals' attacking Babar's cousins. The Africans are dressed in loincloths, have exaggerated red lips, and are attacking the elephants violently. I have to wonder what impact that had on me. The men on this one page surely sent me messages about Africans, or perhaps even a broader POC population, as subhuman, savage, and other."

—Debby Irving, author of *Waking Up White: And Finding Myself in the Story of Race*

"When I think about my childhood with my adult lens, I remember it as incredibly White. However, when I think about it more, I've realized what I really mean is that I wasn't exposed to conversations about race. I remember I used to watch *That's So Raven* and

*(Continued)*

(Continued)

*Sister, Sister* as a child. But my family or friends never talked about the importance of representation on TV. In my English class during junior year, we read *Their Eyes Were Watching God*, which, as an adult, thinking about the pressures that teacher faced in making that selection in a very White town filled with overt racism and vocal parents, I am much more able to appreciate that my White male teacher made that choice. However, this teacher was the only teacher I can recall who explicitly talked about race."

—Lindsay Lyons, educational justice coach, educator, and founder of the educational blog and podcast *Time for Teachership*

"In high school I gained access to BET when it was added to our cable package. I remember being far more interested in and drawn to that station versus MTV and my friends feeling like it was 'weird.' I preferred R&B and soul music and made mixtapes and ordered music in that genre and being called an "N lover" by boys at my high school because of it. This continued into college when for the first time I was around People of Color and began to build friendships with Black people specifically and again received negative feedback from White males about that."

—Melissa Pointer, public school educator and elementary school principal in a school leading the implementation of instruction on race and identity

"I remember the book *The Five Chinese Brothers,* which is written and illustrated by two White people (though I didn't know that at the time). The brothers all look exactly the same and have yellow skin. They don't even have names except [First Chinese Brother], [Second Chinese Brother], etc. Their only individual traits are the unique, superhuman power that each brother possesses. I also remember watching Disney's *Peter Pan* with lines like "We're gonna fight the Injuns" and "Why is the Red Man Red?" song. I also watched *Little House on the Prairie* and remember Laura's family's limited interactions with Native Americans being rooted in, at first, fear, and later on, resentment, for having to leave the land they were living on."

—Rebecca Smoler, English language arts curriculum coordinator for Grades 6-12 in Sharon, Massachusetts; instructor at IDEAS (Initiatives for Developing Equity and Achievement for Students)

---

Reading through these responses, you notice the following themes:

- Mass media representations of people who are not White caused some confusion because these characters were inaccurate, negative, or flat/one-sided depictions.

- Sometimes books and television would lead to a curiosity that was left unsated, undiscussed outside of a small circle (not ever really at home).

- White racial consciousness isn't really a thing for most White people.

---

# Breathe and Reflect

When was the first time you remember seeing and/or reading about people of other races in books, movies, and/or TV shows? Reflect on those books, movies, and/or TV shows. ■

_____

_____

_____

_____

_____

_____

_____

_____

_____

_____

_____

_____

_____

_____

_____

_____

_____

_____

_____

_____

_____

_____

_____

_____

_____

_____

## Ways to Respond

- Consider how you can help students to process the racial implications of what they are reading (both in class-related reading and independent reading) so that they are less likely to form and hold racial misperceptions.

- As you're building relationships with your students, notice what media they enjoy—television shows, TikTok and YouTube videos, music—and if they enjoy media produced by or featuring people who are racially different, try to determine how they are processing their racial differences. Are they receiving negative feedback from peers about their interests? You can do the same with regard to the toys students play with. This will provide you with an opportunity to talk about the joy of appreciating racial diversity, how it differs from cultural appropriation, and how to navigate harmful comments from peers about their interests.

- Notice if the shows and music students enjoy convey harmful, inaccurate messages about certain groups of people, and use this as an opportunity to unpack those messages as well as to teach students to be critical consumers of media.

Growing up, what do you remember your K-12 teachers and/or school doing that clearly showed they didn't understand the history, culture, and oppression of People of Color?

"I was taught, in AP US History, that the Civil War was fought primarily over 'states' rights,' not slavery. I did not learn to question this until college and beyond."

—Sydney Chaffee, teacher of Humanities 9 and instructional coach at Codman Academy Charter Public School, Boston, Massachusetts

"I can clearly remember doing a round robin reading of the book *Brian's Song* in sixth grade and noticing that my passage had the N-word in it. I was so nervous and, when my time to read out loud came, I told my teacher that I didn't feel comfortable reading the passage. She didn't coerce me into reading it but casually asked if someone else would be willing to read it. My classmate Danny read it, N-word and all, and we moved on. But I still remember that so clearly—I even remember what the classroom looked like and where I sat! I don't recall much else other than the absence of stories/works/history of BIPOC until I read *The Autobiography of Malcolm X* for an independent study I did in American Studies my junior year and an elective class I took my senior year that was called 'Minority Literature.'"

—Shawna Coppola, educator, consultant, and author of *Renew: Become a Better and More Authentic Writing Teacher* (2017) and *Writing Redefined: Broadening Our Ideas of What it Means to Compose* (2019)

"I can't remember them doing specific things, it's more about omission. I don't remember learning anything about the history of liberatory action or activism, for example. I always noted that we'd learn about organizing and activism related to the Holocaust, but only learned very fluffy versions of activism related to racial justice in US history."

—Paul Gorski, founder of the Equity Literacy Institute, author of *Reaching and Teaching Students in Poverty* (2013), and coauthor of *Cultivating Social Justice Teachers (2013)* and *Case Studies on Diversity and Social Justice Action* (2013)

"I can now see the complete and total erasure of POC history as well as the erasure of how actual White history and White-told history impacted POC. Add to that the glorification of 'heroes' such as Christopher Columbus, promotion of the level playing field, and strict adherence to the norms of Whiteness, and I can now see the institutional and individual ignorance. At the time, this was just my comfortable normal."

—Debby Irving, author of *Waking Up White, and Finding Myself in the Story of Race*

*(Continued)*

(Continued)

"They never addressed the racism that existed in our schools (from racial slurs to the confederate flags on student trucks in the parking lot) and rarely if ever did a teacher center stories or histories or accomplishments of people who were not White. Teachers who pushed back on this left the school. (I don't know for sure why, but I imagine they were made to leave in some form or another.)"

—Lindsay Lyons, educational justice coach, educator, and founder of the educational blog and podcast *Time for Teachership*

"I remember we went to a campground that had high-ropes/low-ropes courses and we spent three days there as a grade learning about the environment and doing cooperative lessons/activities. The facility was part of the actual Underground Railroad, which is pretty awesome. But I remember one night we had an Underground Railroad activity where teachers were literally pretending to be slave catchers, and we had to move silently from building to building, pretending to be enslaved people trying to get to freedom without being caught. This was done with an all-White staff and at least a 99% White student population. It is mind-blowing to reflect back on. I wonder if my teachers now think back on that lesson with a different perspective."

—Kate LaBelle, Grades 3-6 physical education teacher at Rutland Intermediate School, Vermont

"Since they never talked about race and only focused on the White, European American-centered version of history, it's clear that they either didn't understand the oppression of People of Color or they didn't care."

—Jennifer Wolfrum, graduate instructor and IDEAS (Initiatives for Developing Equity and Achievement for Students) instructor

---

Reading through these responses, you notice the following themes:

- Whitewashed curriculum—teachers didn't understand and/or didn't teach about race

- Developmentally/psychologically inappropriate ways of engaging students about race-based historical occurrences

- Institutional and interpersonal ignoring of racism

---

## Breathe and Reflect

Growing up, what do you remember your K-12 teachers and/or school doing that clearly showed they didn't understand the history, culture, and oppression of People of Color? ■

_____

_____

_____

_____

_____

_____

_____

_____

_____

_____

_____

_____

_____

_____

_____

_____

_____

_____

_____

_____

_____

_____

_____

_____

_____

# Ways to Respond

- Ensure that when you're engaging your students with literary and historical content that you are teaching accurate information.

- Consider how you can include content about cross-racial liberatory work and activism as part of exploring US history.

- If there have been incidents where racial slurs have been used against students in your school community (or the larger community your school is part of), there are racially harmful monuments/flags in your community, and/or there are buildings/streets in your community named after people who have committed actively racist acts, think of ways you can provide students with a way to process these things. Chapter 7 focuses on concrete ways your students can take action against these types of injustices.

- Be sure to engage students in learning experiences about racially difficult topics in developmentally, psychologically, and emotionally appropriate/considerate ways. Be particularly careful about the potential harm that can be done through certain roleplays and reenactments.

If you could go back in time with a magic wand, what changes would you make to your K–12 learning experiences related to people of other races?

"I wish we had read more books by BIPOC authors and learned about contributions and excellence of BIPOC beyond tokens, MLK, Black History Month. I wish my school's 'Diversity Week' was more than a week of White people trying on other cultures' music and dance in the school gym. I wish I had had more teachers and classmates who were not White."

—Sydney Chaffee, teacher of Humanities 9 and instructional coach at Codman Academy Charter Public School, Boston, Massachusetts

"EVERYTHING! I just finished my master's in ABAR education, and what I learned, which people who have been doing this work for DECADES already knew, is that we need to support healthy identity development in all children that honors difference as a strength and disavows notions of superiority and inferiority. AND WE NEED TO TELL CHILDREN THE TRUTH ABOUT THE HISTORY OF THIS PLACE. We also need to uplift and honor the brilliance and resilience of People of the Global Majority who are still here despite calculated attempts at their erasure."

—Marianne Hunkin, educator committed to collective liberation

"I would center non-White stories and histories. I would engage students in conversations about race and racism and White supremacy regularly. I would note the examples of racism in the school community, and I would model critical analysis of things we as students had taken to be acceptable but were examples of racism."

—Lindsay Lyons, educational justice coach, educator, and founder of the educational blog and podcast *Time for Teachership*

"First, I would change the fact that race and identity were never discussed. My experience in schooling was very 'color-blind' and, because we did not openly talk about race, identity, and culture, we missed out on learning about so many of the things that made us all who we are. I also wish I would have learned a more expansive history of this country—like the truth about colonization and mass enslavement, as well as the breadth of abolition and resistance movements. And I wish that I would have been exposed to so many more voices, perspectives, cultural traditions, and lived experiences rather than my education about BIPOC through the limited lens of brutality and exploitation (e.g., land theft, genocide, enslavement) or singular, exceptional—whitewashed—heroes (MLK, Rosa Parks)."

—Carly Riley, director of virtual learning and a facilitator for Embracing Equity

*(Continued)*

(Continued)

"At my MS & HS, I would diversify the schools and staff since research and experience show we all benefit from learning and being surrounded by both people of similar (for affinity) and different (for developing understanding and empathy) backgrounds. K-12, we'd have explicit conversations about identity and race in my classes, where we share strengths/joys and challenges relating to race and other aspects of our identities. The literature and histories that I was taught would include a wide representation of BIPOC voices and experiences—history, identity, culture, & everyday stories, achievements, oppression & struggles. Literature and histories not just in ELA & SS, but all classes."

—Rebecca Smoler, English language arts curriculum
coordinator for Grades 6-12 in Sharon, Massachusetts;
instructor at IDEAS (Initiatives for Developing Equity
and Achievement for Students)

"I'd want my school to be socially justice oriented, helping me to see beyond my child's eye. I think class issues were likely pretty present in my elementary school, but they were never addressed. There probably isn't enough room to write what should have been changed about my high school. It was socially very White dominant, and the school should have done all it could to alter that. In terms of curriculum, I really wasn't paying that much attention, but I know it was a Eurocentric curriculum that left me woefully unprepared to act equitably in a diverse world and racially illiterate as well."

—Shelly Tochluk, author of *Witnessing Whiteness:*
*The Need to Talk About Race and How to Do It* (2010)
and *Living in the Tension: The Quest for a Spiritualized Racial Justice* (2016)

---

Reading through these responses, you notice the following themes:

- Longing for more content about People of Color—and from a nuanced perspective

- Wanting to experience an integrated community and authentic connections with people who were racially different, including teachers

- Wanting to know much earlier that race is a social construct

- Wanting to know about the origins of the land that the United States encompasses

---

## Breathe and Reflect

If you could go back in time with a magic wand, what changes would you make to your K-12 learning experiences related to people of other races? ■

_____

_____

_____

_____

_____

_____

_____

_____

_____

_____

_____

_____

_____

_____

_____

_____

_____

_____

_____

_____

_____

_____

_____

_____

_____

_____

_____

# Ways to Respond

- Take an inventory of the books you use with your students in your instructional practice and the racial backgrounds of the authors of those books. If you find that your books are largely written by and about White people, search for books that are written by and about people from racially marginalized groups. (Many book lists are available online to get you started.)

- If the staff at your school is mostly/all White, find out what efforts your district/school is making to racially diversify the staff, what you can do to support those efforts, and within your locus of control, how you can create opportunities for your students to learn from people outside of their racial identity (e.g., inviting guest speakers in to connect with your students, in person or virtually, from various racial/ethnic backgrounds).

- Explore what is lost by not engaging students with the truth about the history of the United States and the connection to current injustices and inequities. How does that instructional decision hinder students as democratic citizens?

- Build or join a community of White educators who are seeking to learn and implement ABAR instructional practices. Ideally, identify a grade level or content-based colleague to partner within this community so you can support and hold one another accountable.

**If you could go back in time with a magic wand, what changes would you make to your K–12 learning experiences related to being White?**

"I wish I had learned more about Whiteness. I wish my notions of Whiteness as the norm had been challenged. I wish I had known about intersectionality and that someone had been able to help me problematize White feminism, which was so dear to me."

—Sydney Chaffee, teacher of Humanities 9 and instructional
coach at Codman Academy Charter Public
School, Boston, Massachusetts

"I would magically diversify the teaching staff. I wish I had the opportunity to learn from Black people when I was younger and develop those student/mentor relationships. I think that would have impacted me greatly."

—Leigh Ann Erickson, founder of Undone Consulting and Undone Movement; author of
the young adult book *What Is White Privilege?*; educator and developer of the
Connect, Absorb, Respond, and Empower (CARE) curriculum and conference

"I think about this daily. At 33 I am learning about and understanding the lineage of White antiracists. I want children to understand that we do not have to be complicit in upholding White supremacy. That we have ancestors, even if they are not blood ancestors, who chose that path whose stories can fortify us. I want White children to have the language to intervene when injustice happens and for them to be able to dream about a different story for Whiteness. This is healing work, and White people have got to get after it. We can't wait. Our babies cannot wait."

—Marianne Hunkin, educator committed to collective liberation

"I wish that I would have learned about both my own racial identity as well as the construct of Whiteness. I wish that I would have learned about white-skin privilege and the construct of White supremacy—not as the KKK but as a system. And I wish that I would have learned about White activists and abolitionists throughout history who have worked as accomplices and in solidarity to move forward racial justice movements. I think that if us White folx are able to learn about Whiteness as the toxic and harmful construct that it is, then we are less likely to be so fragile when Whiteness/racism is discussed AND we are also more likely to see that we have a role in dismantling it."

—Carly Riley, director of virtual learning and a
facilitator for Embracing Equity

"I'd cast a spell that eliminates the fake history, lies, and partial truths that advance White supremacist thinking—stories that paint people like Columbus and our presidents, such as Washington or Jefferson, as heroes and nothing else. We'd learn our real histories of leaders' participation or complicity with slavery, internment, colonizing, and also learn about antiracist White allies and co-conspirators who pushed back against

*(Continued)*

(Continued)

oppression. I'd want to be taught about racial identity development and what a positive racial identity as a White person could look like. When I first started learning/unlearning about race and racism in our country as an adult, it was especially challenging taking in all of this information while navigating feelings of ignorance and shame. I think the earlier White children can start learning about race/racism/antiracism, the better. I wish I had been given more tools for examining and questioning what I was being taught. Questions I learned from JoAnne Kazis (who is also an Initiatives for Developing Equity and Achievement for Students [IDEAS] instructor) like "Who is telling this story? Whose voice is missing? Who is advantaged by this story? Who is disadvantaged?"

—Rebecca Smoler, English language arts curriculum coordinator
for Grades 6-12 in Sharon, Massachusetts; instructor at IDEAS
(Initiatives for Developing Equity and Achievement for Students)

"I would have my teachers give us the language and words to discuss and understand race, racism, White and settler colonial privilege. And then I would want to have those discussions."

—Jennifer Wolfrum, graduate instructor and IDEAS
(Initiatives for Developing Equity and Achievement for Students) instructor

---

Reading through these responses, you notice the following themes:

- Wanting to learn about intersectionality and White antiracists

- A desire to know more about White identity development earlier

---

## Breathe and Reflect

If you could go back in time with a magic wand, what changes would you make to your K-12 learning experiences related to being White? ∎

_____

_____

_____

_____

_____

_____

_____

_____

_____

_____

_____

_____

_____

_____

_____

_____

_____

_____

_____

_____

_____

_____

_____

_____

_____

_____

_____

_____

_____

_____

# Ways to Respond

- As you engage in this work, realize how your ABAR efforts serve as an antiracist model students can follow, and be willing to be vulnerable and honest with your students about your journey so they can see what's challenging and also what's possible.

- Equip yourself to tell students the truth about US history and current injustices, even when it's hard. By doing this, you will show students what it looks like to persist in the face of resistance.

- Teach students about White antiracist work so that they have a broader perspective about what it can mean to be a White person. Being White does not have to mean being a colonizer or oppressor. With intention, it can mean working for freedom, liberation, and truth for everyone in solidarity with people across our human family.

So what light do all of these personal stories and reflections shine on our own experiences around race—and how have those school experiences shaped our racial identities and our teaching practice? What general themes can we glean from the stories of these White educators and activists? And what specifically can we do in our literacy teaching? These are the themes that jumped out at me while reading the reflections of these colleagues.

Although many of these stories reflect what did and did not take place in social studies and history classes, these experiences have significant implications for our literacy instruction and learning. When we engage students with nonfiction texts and historical fiction, we have the opportunity to present students with an accurate narrative—one that differs from the false and deficit-based narratives that they may have previously encountered or have been influenced by in the media. This may be particularly important for those of us who are humanities teachers. When we blend social studies and literacy instruction or teach social studies directly, we are supporting students to develop critical literacy skills where they continue to move beyond remembering and understanding content to applying, analyzing and evaluating, and laying the foundation for creating something new.

When I reflect on current headlines in the United States, I am convinced that we could all benefit from something new. On February 4, 2022, the Republican National Committee is reported to have stated that the January 6th riot was "legitimate political discourse" (Dawsey & Sonmez 2022). About a week later, a self-professed activist "unwoke" mom hosted a free webinar "to build an army of parents with the skills to torture woke teachers and administrators in schools with mountains of public records requests" (Borysenko 2022). In an attempt to censor what is taught in the classroom, several states would require teachers and administrators to post lesson plans a year in advance, including a list of all books, readings, and activities that teachers use in their lessons. I believe the hope of something better lives in our students, and it's our duty to offer them the building materials needed to make our dreams of freedom, solidarity, and wholeness a reality. In Chapter 2, we'll reflect on how engaging in our own racial identity development is a critical step in that process.

# Starting With Ourselves

## Racial Identity Development for White Educators

My son, Cairo, is left-handed. Everyone else in my family, as far as I know, is right-handed, and at first, I was intrigued by his difference. As someone who is right-handed, however, I did not really know what it was like for Cairo in a world that centers right-handed people.

When Cairo and our daughter, Serena, were young they regularly switched seats in our minivan. Sometimes Cairo would climb into the booster seat and buckle himself in with no problem. At other times, he would say that he couldn't buckle himself in. I found this maddening because we were usually on our way somewhere with some type of time constraint—the pediatrician, a practice or game we had to get to by a certain time—and I would be so frustrated anytime he said he couldn't do it. In my mind, of course he could do it! He had done it before, so why wouldn't he be able to do it again? It took me far too long to realize that he wasn't just saying he couldn't buckle himself in to spice up an otherwise boring ride in the car. When I took the time to wonder why this might be happening, I noticed that when he sat on the right of the car, he could reach up with his left hand, grab the seat belt, pull it across, and buckle himself in with ease because he was using his dominant hand. On days where he had switched seats with Serena and was sitting on the left side of the car, however, he struggled to reach up to buckle himself in with his right hand because that was not his dominant hand.

What if I had taken the time much sooner to be curious and inquire about what Cairo was experiencing? What if I hadn't assumed that I knew what his intentions were? What if I had reflected on the privilege of what it means to be a right-handed person? If someone had asked me back then about the right-handed privilege I enjoyed, I would have struggled to see how I was advantaged, and if someone were to have brought to my attention that I wasn't aware of the challenges left-handed people faced, I may have even said something like "I can't be handist. My son is left-handed." Proximity does not necessarily lead to understanding. Just because you're in a relationship with someone, even a close relationship, doesn't mean you understand their lived experiences. I wasn't aware of my privilege. I was, therefore, not aware of what it felt like to be someone who was not right-handed, like navigating the challenges of writing in a spiral notebook or on a whiteboard; using scissors, can openers, ice cream scoopers, game controllers, computer keyboards; opening refrigerators; trying to eat or work next to a right-handed person without bumping arms; or encountering right-handed desks in classrooms. In my relationship with my son, and by leaning into curiosity and wonder instead of judgment and assumptions, I began to learn.

As a Black, immunocompromised woman whose body is taller, wider, and heavier than what is considered the average body type, I know what it feels like to be marginalized. I also have experienced privilege as an English-speaking, heterosexual, cisgender, able-bodied, Christian, right-handed, college graduate homeowner with a US birth certificate whose family has two cars. During the pandemic, my family also experienced advantages with our access to Wi-Fi with high bandwidth and multiple devices. While working from home, I have experienced the privilege of being someone who lives on the East Coast of the United States, with most meeting times considerate of people who live where I live.

Because of the marginalized aspects of my identity, some of my privileges don't always feel like privileges. For example, although I have a master's degree, I also carry quite a bit of school loan debt, which limits my financial choices. We purchased our first home during the subprime mortgage crisis and had to refinance our mortgage a couple of times to keep from losing our home. Because of the amount of credit card debt we carry as a result of trying to pay for some of our basic needs like car repairs, tuition for our children, and emergency plane tickets, the interest rate on our mortgage is high, which has limited our financial choices as well.

We see the world through the lenses of race, gender, socioeconomic class, religious beliefs, language, age, ability, citizenship, education, and employment stage. We are also influenced by our personalities, likes, dislikes, interests, and position in our families, and, as I mentioned in the beginning of this chapter, our dominant hands. Some parts of our identities are more salient than others. Although I wasn't as aware of the privileged parts of my identity in the past, including being right-handed when it could have been helpful to my son, I am more aware now, and when you know better, you do better.

# STAGES OF WHITE RACIAL IDENTITY

Awareness of the impact of our identities and lived experiences across differences is an integral part of our racial consciousness journeys and racial identity development—our journey toward doing better. Unless we had a unique childhood, this is not an experience that most of us have had as we grew up in the United States, so it's work we need to do now in order to be our full selves and to best support our students.

Beverly Daniel-Tatum, PhD, president emerita of Spelman College, psychologist, and author of *"Why Are All the Black Kids Sitting Together in the Cafeteria?" and Other Conversations About Race* (2017b) explores racial identity development in her work. In a 2020 interview with the Parents League of New York, she shared that young People of Color usually begin to develop a racial/ethnic identity in adolescence as they begin to see themselves through the eyes of others. For White people, it is possible for the process to also begin in adolescence, unless they live in predominantly White, segregated communities. In that case, the racial/ethnic identity development begins much later. "For them," Daniel-Tatum states, "being White is just 'being normal' like everyone else, and that dimension of identity goes unnoticed and undiscussed most of the time. For that reason, many White adults who live and work in predominantly White environments have given little consideration to the meaning of their own racial group membership" (Parents League of New York 2020).

What, then, does racial identity development look like for a White adult in the United States? How does one begin to develop a racial identity when one has lived in a predominantly White community for decades? Janet Helms studied racial identity development and explored the concept in *A Race Is a Nice Thing to Have: A Guide to Being a White Person or Understanding the White Persons in Your Life* (2008), which includes the following stages for people who identify as White: contact, disintegration, reintegration, pseudo-independence, immersion/emersion, and autonomy (see Figure 2.1). Let's dig into these concepts further.

**Contact:** Folks in the contact stage have a "color-blind" approach to race, a perspective that talking about racial difference and believing that race is an issue is what causes racism, and do not tend to commit explicitly racist acts. Those in this stage can harbor racist beliefs that are harder to detect because of their refusal to see race, and when confronted with race-based incidents where the advantages of having White skin are revealed, can move into the disintegration stage. Someone in this stage may say things like the following:

- *There is only one race—the human race.*
- *The United States is a melting pot.*
- *We are a nation of immigrants.*
- *All lives matter!*

FIGURE 2.1   Stages of White Identity Development

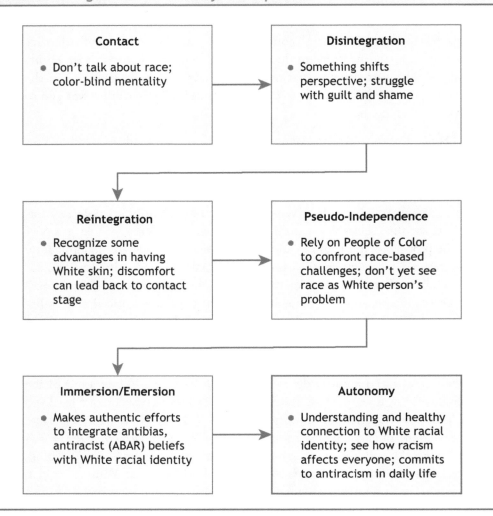

**Contact**
- Don't talk about race; color-blind mentality

**Disintegration**
- Something shifts perspective; struggle with guilt and shame

**Reintegration**
- Recognize some advantages in having White skin; discomfort can lead back to contact stage

**Pseudo-Independence**
- Rely on People of Color to confront race-based challenges; don't yet see race as White person's problem

**Immersion/Emersion**
- Makes authentic efforts to integrate antibias, antiracist (ABAR) beliefs with White racial identity

**Autonomy**
- Understanding and healthy connection to White racial identity; see how racism affects everyone; commits to antiracism in daily life

**Disintegration:** People in this stage have new experiences and/or learn something new that begins to shift their perspectives about race-related matters, and they struggle with guilt and shame because they begin to see that their previous perspective was based on false narratives and/or incomplete information. This can be a foundation on which a person begins to build ABAR beliefs and move to the reintegration stage.

Someone in this stage may say things like the following:

- *I didn't realize that redlining kept Black people from owning homes.*

- *I didn't understand how some People of Color felt about the police until I saw the recording of George Floyd's murder.*

- *If someone like Serena Williams can experience inferior health care after the birth of her child, perhaps there are systemic inequities in the health care system.*

- *I believed what was said about the young Black men who were accused of assaulting the Central Park jogger being super-predators, but it turns out they were falsely accused.*

**Reintegration:** People in this stage might blame people from marginalized groups for the challenges they face. While experiencing reintegration, there may be a belief that the advantages that come along with having White skin are deserved. If someone in this stage is able to overcome these feelings, they may transition into the pseudo-independence stage.

Someone in this stage may say/ask things like the following:

- *Look at the rioters burning down their own community.*

- *What about Black on Black crime?*

- *If you think the United States is so bad, you should leave!*

- *I have experienced reverse racism.*

- *If you haven't done anything wrong, you have nothing to fear from the police.*

**Pseudo-independence:** Someone in this stage may look to People of Color to confront race-based challenges. They don't see it as their work but are supportive of the work being done, which affirms their view of themselves as not being racist. This is the first stage of positive racial identification, though the person has yet to connect with being White and becoming an active antiracist.

Someone in this stage may do things like the following:

- *Remain silent during race-based discussions/ interaction but send private messages to or talk with People of Color individually to express support.*

- *Support the hiring of People of Color to "increase diversity" for junior-level positions but not for leadership roles.*

- *Support "inclusion" efforts so that People of Color have a seat at an already established table but not with decision-making power.*

- *Support People of Color who kneel during the national anthem in protest of the shootings/ killings of unarmed People of Color, but not kneel themselves.*

It's important to consider the impact that pseudo-independence has on People of Color. Neil A. Lester's (2017) article, "For White Allies in Search of a Solution to Racism/When Folks of Color Are Exhausted," offers guidance for people who find themselves in this stage.

https://bit.ly/3v6Uxxh

**Immersion/emersion:** Here, one exhibits authentic efforts to integrate ABAR beliefs with their White racial identity, especially by developing relationships with other White people who are engaging in ABAR practices.

Someone in this stage may do things like the following:

- *Participate in a protest against race-based injustices.*

- *Participate in a book club where a book about race is discussed.*

- *Attend equity sessions at conferences.*

- *Join a White affinity group with an antiracist focus.*

- *Sign petitions in support of equitable and just racial practices.*

**Autonomy:** At this stage, one develops an understanding of and healthy connection to their White racial identity, sees how systemic racism affects everyone, and is a committed and active antiracist.

Someone in this stage may do things like the following:

- *Educate themselves on the positions that political candidates support that have racial implications before voting and allow that information to shape their vote.*

- *Advocate for affordable housing efforts in their communities.*

- *Speak up against an injustice instead of waiting for People of Color to address it.*

- *Speak up in favor of ABAR instructional practices at school board meetings.*

- *Donate to Indigenous organizations and are aware of the history of the land they live and work on.*

## Breathe and Reflect

If you identify as White, what stage of racial identity development do you find yourself in currently? What have you noticed that makes you place yourself there? What resonates with you from that stage? Is there a shift you'd like to make? ■

_____

_____

_____

_____

_____

_____

_____

_____

_____

_____

_____

_____

_____

_____

_____

_____

_____

_____

_____

_____

_____

_____

_____

_____

_____

_____

It's important to be aware of one's own racial identity development to avoid going from being unaware of systemic injustices to believing that the way to address them is to try to help people who you believe are less fortunate than you are instead of seeing how systemic oppression negatively impacts all of us. Without healthy racial identity development and a full and accurate understanding of history, you can begin to think that it's your responsibility to save people from marginalized groups instead of realizing that we *all* need saving from the consequences of racism. Without healthy racial identity development, you may find yourself pitying People of Color, for example, or adopting a deficit perspective and assigning blame for the challenges they experience—a mindset that is indicative of the reintegration stage of White identity development—instead of working to dismantle the systems that created the challenges in the first place.

## THE DANGER OF DEFICIT THINKING

Let's look at a specific example of how lack of full understanding of racial identity can lead to deficit thinking models—and then in the next section we'll wrestle with how to rework some of this wiring in our own thinking. Consider the work of Ruby Payne, for example, who is best known for her book *A Framework for Understanding Poverty* (2018; now in its sixth edition). Payne's work delves into what she calls the *culture of poverty* and how she believes it impacts education. However, Payne's perspective is an example of a deficit perspective about people experiencing poverty. She writes about the symptoms of poverty without interrogating the causes. Unfortunately, there are a number of schools and districts that have used and are using Payne's work to inform their perspectives about and approaches to how they perceive and work with students and families who are experiencing poverty.

In *A Framework for Understanding Poverty*, for example, Payne (2005) lists survival skills needed by different societal classes. The section about surviving in poverty includes survival skills like *I know how to*:

- Locate grocery stores' garbage bins that have thrown-away food.
- Bail someone out of jail.
- Physically fight and defend myself.
- Get a gun, even if I have a police record.
- Keep my clothes from being stolen at a laundromat.
- Sniff out problems in a used car.
- Live without a checking account.
- Get around without a car.

These statements are problematic on so many levels, filled with stereotypes and assumptions. For example, people who are considerate of the impact of harmful emissions may take public transportation or ride bikes, regardless of their socio-economic status, so people who are experiencing poverty are not the only people who can get around without a car. My family washed our clothes in a laundromat before my parents were in a financial position to buy a washer and dryer for our apartment, and my family was never concerned about our clothes being stolen. I wonder about the use of the word *sniff*, too, as it evokes images of animals instead of humans. Aren't there many reasons why someone would choose not to have a checking account? And I know there are people in the middle and wealthy classes who know how to bail someone out of jail.

The section about surviving in the middle class includes statements about getting children to Little League, piano lessons, and soccer; ordering comfortably in a nice restaurant; getting the best interest rate on a car loan; getting a library card; decorating the house for holidays; and talking to children about going to college. The section about surviving in wealth includes statements like having favorite restaurants in countries around the world, having at least two homes that are staffed and maintained, knowing how to enroll your children in preferred private schools, and supporting the work of a particular artist. Are these things true? And if they are, is it because people who are experiencing poverty don't want these things for themselves and their families, or is it that they don't have access?

When we examine this example, the problems with deficit thinking become clearer. There is avoidance in assigning blame to people in underserved, underrepresented populations—or simply throwing our hands in the air and saying, "That's just the way it is"—instead of recognizing our role in sustaining or dismantling the systems that created the imbalance.

## BE OPEN TO PRODUCTIVE STRUGGLE WITH RACIAL IDENTITY

We know as educators that if students try to move from confusion to understanding without experiencing the challenge of the process, they are not really learning. The same is true for us as adults and is particularly important to consider when it comes to racial identity and consciousness development. We need to engage in the same productive struggle that we encourage our students to engage in as they're learning something new. We can embrace this process as it relates to our own learning and growth by developing our emotional intelligence (also known as EQ, or emotional quotient).

In her book *Onward: Cultivating Emotional Resilience in Educators*, Elena Aguilar (2018) encourages us to engage in critical work as we develop our emotional intelligence practices, including knowing ourselves, understanding emotions, building community, cultivating compassion, being a learner, and riding the waves of change. Each of these practices is essential to laying a strong foundation as we interrupt systems of oppression as they show up in our learning spaces. This work is hard, and the temptation to maintain the status quo is strong, so we must be aware of the potential pitfalls we may face. Systems of inequity are formidable foes.

https://bit.ly/3K9b4oq

A major aspect of productive struggle with racial identity is understanding how we have been racially socialized. In "White Supremacy Culture Characteristics: The Characteristics of White Supremacy Culture" from *Dismantling Racism: A Workbook for Social Change Groups*, Okun (n.d.) defines thirteen characteristics that are present in our culture.

In my experience, here's how five of these characteristics can show up in this work in schools, in particular, and create barriers to our progress if we're not careful:

- *Perfectionism:* Failing to engage meaningfully in race-related work for fear of making mistakes

- *Sense of urgency:* Not taking into consideration that racism and systems of oppression have evolved over centuries and that there are no quick fixes in this work

- *Defensiveness:* Believing that if someone's intentions are good, not being open to having their thoughts, feelings, experiences, or choices challenged without triggering a strong self-protective reaction that typically centers the wants of that person instead of progress toward collective healing and benefit

- *Fear of open conflict:* Having a strong aversion to strong, public emotions/emotional displays, especially if one feels blamed or perceived as responsible for the source of those emotions

- *Right to comfort:* Showing up as people wanting to engage in work that focuses more on general diversity and inclusion matters—those that typically veer away from race

All of these characteristics divert us from the work of liberation and are evidence of the fact that we, as a society, need healing.

## Breathe and Reflect

What do you feel when reflecting on and engaging with race-related topics? Which of the emotional intelligence practices do you want to lean into now? What connections do you notice to any of the five White supremacy culture characteristics named above? Take some time to write or record what you notice. ■

_____

_____

_____

_____

_____

_____

_____

_____

_____

_____

_____

_____

_____

_____

_____

_____

_____

_____

_____

_____

_____

_____

_____

_____

_____

# THE NEED FOR HEALING FROM RACIALIZATION

In the summer of 2019, I had the opportunity to speak at and participate in the White Responsibility Anti Racism Teach-In and to learn from some of the people who had most influenced my learning about race and education; being in the company of thought leaders like Jacqueline Battalora, Zaretta Hammond, Liza Talusan, and Ijeoma Oluo transformed me. The teach-in deepened my understanding of race as a social construct as well as the vital connection between culturally responsive teaching and the liberation that comes with effective literacy instruction and provided tools to support productive conversations about race.

Explore the resources based on California Newsreel's documentary series *Race: The Power of an Illusion* (https://newsreel.org/guides/race/pressreleasecredit.htm) about race in society, science, and history to learn more about the origins, beliefs, and consequences of what we call "race." There are resources to help you to learn more about what race is, whether or not you can tell someone's race by looking at them, how ideas about race have changed over time, human diversity and how different are we really, how race impacts our daily lives, and how race has impacted housing in the United States.

https://bit.ly/3MnS8nt

During the teach-in, one of the presenters shared an image of a Dove Summer Glow Nourishing Body Lotion. The image showed that the product was made for people with "normal to dark skin." There was an audible gasp from other participants, which caused cognitive dissonance for me. I didn't gasp. I didn't see anything out of the ordinary in that image, but clearly, there was something upsetting to other participants, so I looked at the image again. And that's when I saw it. *Normal to dark skin. Normal to dark skin.* Dark skin is not considered normal.

Why hadn't I noticed the problem with the product as soon as I saw it? It became clear to me that I needed to heal from something deep inside, and it had to do with oppression.

There are four interlocking aspects of oppression that build on and support each other: ideological, institutional, interpersonal, and internalized (see Figure 2.2). Any effort to end oppression should address all four levels.

**Ideological:** This is the false narrative that one group of people is better than another. There is a privileged group that attributes positive characteristics to itself and a group that is disadvantaged and assigned negative characteristics.

*Example:* The belief that White and Asian people are more intelligent and hardworking than Black people.

FIGURE 2.2   Interlocking Aspects of Oppression

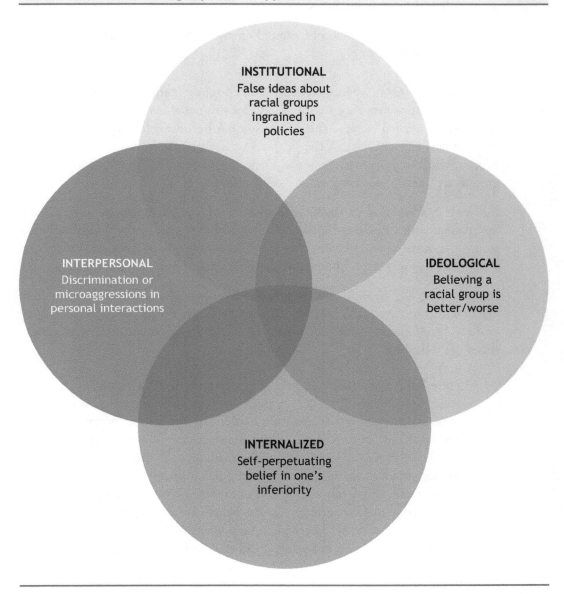

**Institutional:** This is how false ideas about groups of people become ingrained in the practices and policies of our health care, legal, housing, economic, political, educational, media, entertainment, employment, and other systems. When these false ideas become institutionalized, we see evidence of disadvantaged and marginalized groups being denied equitable, fair, and just access to these systems.

*Example:* White women earn $0.82 for every dollar non-Hispanic White men earn, but Black women earn $0.63 for the same (and even less in some states).

**Interpersonal:** This is how bias, discrimination, prejudice, and stereotyping show up in individual and group interactions.

*Example:* Saying to a Person of Color, "When I look at you, I don't see color" or "You're so articulate!"

**Internalized:** This is when historically and currently marginalized people believe the false narrative that they are inferior. Once this belief is internalized, individual actors aren't needed because the oppression has become self-perpetuating. It has become part of the DNA of the people in these groups. You don't, for example, need to tell your fingernails to grow. They just do because the directions for that growth are already programmed at a cellular level.

*Example:* My reaction (or lack thereof) to the Dove ad represents internalized oppression, which can show up as internalized inferiority, just as a White person seeing the same ad and not noticing anything wrong would indicate internalized superiority or supremacy. Both reactions show evidence of a need for healing.

In his book, *My Grandmother's Hands* (Menakem 2017), Resmaa Menakem explores the concept of White supremacy as a trauma response—not simply an attitude, belief system, or way of seeing the world. In a *Medium* article, Menakem states the following:

> White Supremacy—and all the claims, accusations, excuses, and dodges that surround it—are a trauma response. This response lives not inside psyches, but deep within bodies. (In fact, a more accurate term for the affliction is *white-body supremacy*, since it elevates the white body above all other bodies. The white body is the ostensibly supreme standard against which other bodies' humanity is measured.) The attitudes, convictions, and beliefs of white-body supremacy are reflexive cognitive side effects, like the belief of a claustrophobe that the walls are closing in. These ideas have been reinforced through institutions as practice, procedures, and standards. (Menakem 2014)

An example of how this shows up is the volume and frequency of media coverage regarding Gabby Petito, a young White woman who went missing and was later found murdered in September 2021, compared to the consistent lack of coverage about missing, murdered Women of Color, particularly Indigenous women. How we typically respond to the ideas and impact of White supremacy has been ineffective up until this point. If we acknowledge White supremacy as a trauma response, however, we can address it more effectively as a condition for which we all need healing.

## Breathe and Reflect

Of the four types of oppression, which one do you find yourself wanting to learn more about? Use this space to reflect on what has captured your attention and any connections to what you've noticed about how White bodies are treated, as Menakem says, as a supreme standard. ■

_____

_____

_____

_____

_____

_____

_____

_____

_____

_____

_____

_____

_____

_____

_____

_____

_____

_____

_____

_____

_____

_____

_____

_____

_____

# Uncovering, Dismantling, and Healing From Racialization

I had the privilege of leading a group of my colleagues from a variety of racial and ethnic backgrounds through a ten-week discussion of *The Racial Healing Handbook* by Anneliese Singh (2019). Though some of the questions in the book involved recalling painful experiences and were challenging to consider, it was such a powerful and beneficial experience. I didn't have a true appreciation of the depth of the wound racialization had caused in my person, and reading the book and engaging with the activities was like a balm for that wound. Other participants in the book discussion shared that they had a similar experience. It's vital for us to engage in this healing work if we have any hope of beginning the journey of recovering from the impact of racialization and offering our students a better way of being.

Although I encourage you to purchase this book and do the work Singh leads us through, the following are some of the questions from that work that have immediate implications for educators. I encourage you to use these reflection questions, based on Singh's (2019) book, to guide your journey toward uncovering, dismantling, and healing from racialization. (See the responses from educators in Chapter 1 and in the online companion, as well as the Letters to My Younger Self in the online companion.)

1. **Knowing my racial identity:** Examining what we needed to know about race when we were growing up can guide us in offering those learnings and experiences to our students now. These questions can guide this inquiry:

   - *What did I need to know about my race when I was growing up? How would these things have changed my earliest memories of race and racism?*

   - *What were the racial scripts of the people who raised me?*

   - *When did I begin to notice race?*

   - *What reinforcements of racial socialization—rewards for playing along or punishments for stepping outside of racial scripts—did I experience, and what were the dehumanizing results?*

It is important for teachers to be aware of how we've all been socialized and the racial scripts we and our students are operating by as well as to ensure that we are not dehumanizing anyone with our policies, and instructional practices.

2. **Exploring my internalized racism:** Taking the time to resocialize ourselves racially better equips us to create and sustain healthy learning communities for our students. These questions can guide this self-reflection:

   - *What is the world I needed to see when I was a child?*

   - *What did I need the adults in my life to teach me?*

- *What are the institutional and cultural messages I needed to hear?*
- *What positive reinforcements would have benefited me, and what could have been different with a healthier race socialization?*
- *How can I resocialize my racial self?*

3. **Learning and unlearning racism:** Being aware of where we need to engage in more learning can help us to be aware of the gaps in what we can offer our students instructionally. The following questions can help form this awareness:

- *What is my personal lesson plan on the history of racism?*
- *How would I rate myself now on my own knowledge of the history of racism?*
- *Think about the knowledge I have about the following groups, and rank from 1 (a lot of knowledge) to 3 (very little knowledge):*
  - Alaska Native/First Nations/Indigenous People/Native Americans
  - Asian/Pacific Islander Americans
  - Black/African Americans
  - Latinx/o/a/ Hispanic Americans
  - Middle Eastern Americans
  - White/European Americans

4. **Grieving and naming racism:** When we are aware of what stage(s) of grief we and our students are experiencing as a result of race-based incidents in our lives, we can better prepare to support students effectively. Ask yourself these questions to grapple with this process:

- *What is a recent experience with racism? What did it feel like? How did I respond?*
- *Can I apply the five stages of grief to my experiences with racism (denial, anger, bargaining, depression, acceptance)?*

5. **Raising my race consciousness:** Educators must be aware of how we respond to taking risks related to ABAR instructional practices. This work takes courage, and noting where we are strong can help to build a scaffold for the areas needing growth. Reflect on these questions:

- *How am I becoming antiracist?*
- *How do I take risks to challenge racism when I see it or realize when I am participating in it?*
- *What are my strengths in this area and what are my areas that need growth?*

6. **Catching yourself in the flow of racism:** Being aware of how we respond to (or inflict!) microaggressions that occur in our classroom and/or school can help us to take a more proactive approach so that we are more prepared to respond effectively when the microaggressions occur instead of fleeing, freezing, fighting, or appeasing. Ask yourself these questions:

- *How can I delve deeper into personal experiences of racial microaggressions?*
- *What is my most often experienced racial microaggression?*
- *How does this most often manifest?*
- *What is my typical internal response?*
- *How can I refine my typical internal dialogue so I don't internalize racism?*

7. **Understanding racism in relationships:** Identifying the messages we received in school can help us to be more mindful of the messages our students receive from us and the school community as a whole. With that knowledge, we can work to ensure that the messages students receive about their own race and the race of others are healthy messages that authentically support what we say we believe. Ask yourself these questions:
   - *How does race and racism show up in school?*
   - *What were the main messages I learned in school about my own race and the race of others?*

8. **Reclaiming your whole racial self:** Being aware of the intersectional aspects of ABAR instructional practices can better prepare us for the nuances and complexities of this work. Here are some guiding questions:
   - *What are my intersecting identities of privilege and oppression?*
   - *How do I think my (dis)ability intersects with my race?*

9. **Becoming a racial ally:** Examining the challenges of allyship can help us to be more strategic and proactive when it comes to supporting our students to be upstanders. Reflect on this:
   - *What were three times when it was tough to be a racial ally?*

10. **Engaging in collective racial healing:** Thinking about the aspects of creating a healthy community can help us to create such a community with our students. Consider these questions:
    - *What is my relationship to community?*
    - *What is the foundation of healthy communities I'm part of?*
    - *What are the rewards of being in community?*

11. **Dreaming of what a racially just world looks like:** Writing down our next steps and developing an accountability plan helps us to move toward making our dream of a racially just world a reality. Here are questions to help you form your plan:
    - *What are my next steps?*
    - *How can I continue to grow as an antiracist?*
    - *How do I hold myself accountable?*

Anneliese Singh shared on the Abolitionist Teaching Network's *Teaching to Thrive* podcast, when discussing how we heal from racism, that

> . . . racial healing is when we take the time to really do that life inventory, that we go back and we . . . reconnect with that little kid that is in all of us that just learned such lies about race and racism, and we scoop that little kid up if you're White and say, "Sweetie, whew, that was a big lie, and we've got some work to do. And sometimes you're going to feel guilty and ashamed, and wish you would've known better, and I'm going to be right there along with you as your loving adult and we're going to move through those emotions and we're going to reclaim our humanity." (Love and Culley-Love 2021, 41:31–42:03).

One goal of this book is to walk alongside you through this process for your own healing and development as an educator and to equip you to support your students through the same process.

Although race is a social construct, it has significant meaning and power in our society. In order to equip White students as global citizens, teachers need to both learn about and teach students about the contact, disintegration, reintegration, pseudo-independence, immersion/emersion, and autonomy stages of White racial identity development, as well as the impact of Whiteness, racialization, and privilege on relationships, communities, power, access, and systems.

We have to be willing to give ourselves the learning experiences that we should have participated in our K–12 experiences and in our undergraduate and postgraduate learning experiences. Although this process won't necessarily lead to a degree, it will equip you with the ability to truly be the teachers our students deserve.

As Daniel Hill (2020) states, "I believe there is an opportunity for White folks to experience our own version of liberation from white supremacy. But we have to believe we are damaged to experience that liberation. Currently, only a minority of White folks actually believe this" (48). The following reflection questions are designed to support you as you begin to write/record your own racial autobiography. There's a link to my racial autobiography recording, which includes the questions that guided my exploration, in the online companion to this book.

# Breathe and Reflect

Think back to when you were five, six, or seven years old, and reflect on your earliest memories of race. Reflections can focus on personal interactions with or about people from other racial groups and what you saw (or didn't see) on TV shows, on cartoons, in movies, in books, at the supermarket, at the mall, on vacations, with toys, in advertisements, in magazines, at camp, at places of worship, on teams, at school, and so on. Use this reflection to begin to write or record your own racial autobiography, and consider how you can help your students to do the same. ■

_____

_____

_____

_____

_____

_____

_____

Take an inventory of the voices that inform your ideas, preferences, beliefs, and opinions. Who are your neighbors, friends, and authority figures? What news sources do you rely on? Who are the authors of the majority of the books you read? Who are the stars of the TV shows and movies you watch? If you have a place of worship, is there a racial majority group? How have these parts of your life changed or remained the same over time? Use this reflection to begin to create your own racial journey map, and consider how you can help your students to do the same. ■

_____

_____

_____

_____

_____

_____

_____

_____

# CHAPTER 3

# Instructional Strategies That Help Students Develop Racial Identities and Understandings

During my elementary teaching graduate program, I worked as a full-time building aide at a school in an affluent suburb outside of Boston. Most of the students at the school identified as Jewish, though there were Black and Brown students who were bussed to the district from Boston through the Metropolitan Council for Educational Opportunity (METCO) voluntary desegregation program. I spent most of my time in a fifth-grade classroom so that when the teacher was away participating in literacy training throughout the year, I would take over as the substitute teacher.

I appreciated the opportunity to work with these students, especially after an incident during a reading workshop. The teacher read *The Great Gilly Hopkins* (Paterson 1978), and when we got to the part of the book where Gilly, the main character, insinuates the N-word in reference to her Black teacher, the students were confused (the reference is meant to rhyme with the word *figger*, though Gilly never actually uses the N-word). Instead of answering the question herself, the teacher asked if I wanted to explain. I declined her invitation—this was her class, and she had been the one who decided to read this book to them. I felt a mix of emotions—surprise at being put on the spot, disappointment that she was unprepared to discuss this content with her students, and resentment that she was choosing to avoid having this important conversation with her students and attempting to put all the weight of this conversation on me.

I know now that her response was indicative of someone at the pseudo-independence stage of White identity development. The teacher apologized after class for attempting to pass the question on to me, and in that conversation I realized that although the school had a commitment to antibias, antiracist (ABAR) instructional practices, and each teacher was required to participate in what was then Empowering Multicultural Initiatives (EMI) and now Initiatives for Developing Equity and Achievement for Students (IDEAS) coursework, that didn't guarantee that all teachers were ready to have conversations about race with students. Although I was in her classroom to learn from her, I realized how symbiotic the relationship between student teacher and cooperating teacher actually needed to be.

During one of the teacher's weeks away, I engaged the students in conversation about challenging topics related to race. Today, educators have access to supportive tools like Learning for Justice's "Teaching Hard History" resources for students in Grades K–5 and 6–12. But in the absence of such resources, I created and shared a questionnaire with the students to determine what their opinions were about a variety of race-related topics. One of the questions was "Do you believe that the descendants of enslaved Africans in the United States deserve reparations for enslavement?" One student, who identified as White, adamantly responded, "No—my family and I never owned slaves, and I don't think we should have to be responsible for what someone else did." I asked him a follow-up question: "Do you believe that Holocaust survivors and the descendants of those who were killed during the Holocaust deserved reparations for the Holocaust?" He said yes. I asked him what was the difference for him, and I could see his mind navigating through confusion, uncertainty, and budding awareness. He said he didn't know.

What I knew, though, and what he and his classmates were able to begin to consider, is that we feel connected to and empathetic toward those whose stories we relate to, understand, and feel impacted by. That student had done some reading and study of the Holocaust and World War II themes and maybe even had familial or cultural connections to survivors, so it was easier for him to make the connection to reparations for those whose families were affected directly by the Holocaust. Without a firm understanding about race in the United States, however, he struggled to connect and find empathy for the descendants of enslaved Africans.

This is an example of what can happen when students don't have the opportunity to develop an understanding of their own racial identity and how it impacts how they see themselves and the world. As Figure 1.1 in Chapter 1 showed, all children have been exposed to mostly White children in their children's books and have learned from Eurocentric, White-dominant curricula. For White students, being surrounded by mirrors results in a lack of understanding and empathy for the experiences of people in traditionally marginalized groups.

# Breathe and Reflect

Can you think of examples of times in your teaching experience when it became clear that your students struggled with understanding or empathizing with people who didn't share their racial identity? Use this space to capture that experience. ▪

_____

_____

_____

_____

_____

_____

_____

_____

_____

_____

_____

_____

_____

_____

_____

_____

_____

_____

_____

_____

_____

_____

_____

_____

_____

# THE IMPACT OF SEGREGATION ON WHITE CHILDREN

In Chapter 2, we explored the stages of White racial identity development. The first three stages can be characterized by substantial challenges—particularly color blindness at the contact stage, shame and guilt at the disintegration stage, and fear and anger toward People of Color at the reintegration phase. Our segregated communities contribute to these challenges because we don't always have the opportunity to live in neighborhoods and to form meaningful relationships with people who are racially different. Throughout modern history, there are examples of how segregation, whether social or state-enforced, hurts everyone, including White people. Heather McGhee (2021), in *The Sum of Us,* tells the story of the Oak Park pool in Mississippi in 1959. When a federal court decision deemed segregated recreational spaces unconstitutional, the Oak Park City Council decided to drain the pool rather than integrate it. This practice took place at countless pools across the country and is a topic that is explored in the picture book *Freedom Summer* by Deborah Wiles (2005): the story of a Black boy and White boy who, though friends and excited to finally have the chance to swim together in the town pool, were not able to because the town filled the pool in with tar rather than have it integrated. McGhee writes about the impact not only on Black residents but on White people—particularly confused White children who wept as cement was poured into the pool.

Though this occurred over sixty years ago, we still face the same challenges. While segregated pools may no longer be an issue (in law if not always in practice, as evidenced by incidents like the one in 2018 in a Winston-Salem, North Carolina, neighborhood where a White neighbor asked his Black neighbor and her son to show identification to prove she lived in the neighborhood when she tried to access the community pool), we are still a largely segregated society. McGhee (2021) writes,

> This is one of those truths that we Americans know without a doubt and yet like to deny: Who your neighbors, co-workers, and your classmates are is one of the most powerful determinants of your path in life. And most [W]hite Americans spend their lives on a path set out for them by a centuries-old lie: that in the zero-sum racial competition, [W]hite spaces are the best spaces. White people are the most segregated people in America.
>
> The typical [W]hite person lives in a neighborhood that is at least 75% [W]hite. In today's increasingly multiracial society, where [W]hite people value diversity but rarely live it, there are costs—financial, developmental, even physical—to continuing to segregate as we do. (168–169)

Consider what this means in our public schools as well: If White students live in White neighborhoods, they attend schools with mostly White students and teachers and learn from a White-centric curriculum. What does this mean for these students? I find it interesting that, as educators, we are comfortable using terms like *at risk* and *high needs* when talking about students and communities of color, but we don't consider the need and risk that exist for White students living in segregated communities who don't have access to ABAR instruction and lived experiences. We don't often talk about the historical and current impact of racialization on the minds and lives of White children.

McGhee also explores an essential and often overlooked consideration regarding the *Brown v. Board of Education of Topeka* decision in 1954. In addition to asserting the importance of bringing an end to the unequal access and resources, and feeling of inferiority experienced by Black children caused by segregation, the case also detailed the harm segregation inflicts on White children. McGhee (2021) writes,

> The best research of the day concluded that "confusion, conflict, moral cynicism, and disrespect for authority may arise in [White] children as a consequence of being taught the moral, religious and democratic principles of justice and fair play by the same persons and institutions who seem to be acting in a prejudiced and discriminatory manner." (183)

When we take into consideration the reality of how segregation has persisted in our communities across the country, we must contemplate the impact on our students and their racial identity development. Integrating our communities isn't something that will happen immediately. What we can do, however, is ensure that our students have the opportunity to gaze through windows to learn about people with different racial identities until all of our communities reflect the racial diversity that we espouse. And we can help our White students understand and develop their own sense of racial identity so that their fear and shame around race conversations can dissipate.

As educators, we can provide students with the opportunities to grapple with the history and current impact of segregation by laying a foundation of racial identity discovery on which the curiosity about the racial identity of others can grow. This will involve connecting your racial journey work with students' identity formation, helping students understand the complexity of identity, supporting students to build empathy, and connecting their White identity development with their identity as someone committed to ABAR ways of being.

# Breathe and Reflect

What do you notice about the impact of segregated communities on you and your students? What is the impact of not having the opportunity to share space with people who are racially different? ■

_____

_____

_____

_____

_____

_____

_____

_____

_____

_____

_____

_____

_____

_____

_____

_____

_____

_____

_____

_____

_____

_____

_____

_____

_____

_____

Chapter 2 provided the tools and invited you to engage in your own racial identity work and capture your racial story. In this chapter, you will learn how to invite students to do the same in a developmentally appropriate, accessible way. You can provide the support your students need to begin to engage in their own exploration of their racial selves as part of their literacy development work. I encourage you to engage with these exercises, too, and invite colleagues to do the same. Let's now take a look at examples of instructional moves you can make with your students at the upper elementary and secondary levels as they develop their own racial identities.

## AFFIRMING IDENTITY BY EXPLORING WHAT HAS SHAPED US

Helping students to develop positive identities involves providing them with the opportunity to explore the different aspects of who they are and what has shaped who they are becoming. In addition to having different racial/cultural backgrounds, physical and artistic abilities, and varying identities along a gender spectrum, your students are people with different likes, preferences, interests, and personalities—they are introverted, extroverted, shy, gregarious, curious, playful, creative, bold, and cautious. We are all shaped by our families and communities and also by who we are at our core.

### WRITING "WHERE I'M FROM" POEMS

Whether you are teaching students to analyze literary devices and content in reading or learning to use mentor texts to create their own literary pieces, George Ella Lyon's poem, "Where I'm From" (1993), inspired by Tennessee writer Jo Carson's *Stories I Ain't Told Nobody Yet* (1993), provides an excellent opportunity to help students explore the different parts of their identities.

https://bit.ly/3vCSDn1

In this poem, Lyon explores the people, traditions, sights, sounds, tastes, ways of being, and memories that compose who she is.

Here's how this activity might look in your classroom:

- Read the poem with your students, go to GeorgeEllaLyon.com, and click the *Where I'm From* tab to listen to Lyon read the poem herself.

- Discuss the poem as a group, asking students to pay specific attention to and then list what they notice and wonder about Lyon as they read and listen to her poem.

- Model some of these noticings and wonderings before students create their own lists independently, and then compare and contrast their lists with one another in small groups. For example:

| I NOTICE . . . | I WONDER . . . |
|---|---|
| Lyon mentions laundry-related items like clothespins and Clorox. | Who are Imogene, Alafair, Artemus, and Billie? |
| She spent time under her back porch. | What does a Dutch elm look like? |
| Lyon mentions several tastes, like beets, fried corn, and fudge. | What is an auger? |

- Once students have spent time engaging with the poem, support them as they create their own.

This strategy is most effective if you have first written and shared your own "Where I'm From" poem with students and modeled how and why you chose what to include in your poem. Share your poem(s) with your students as a way to build relationships and to model what you'll support them to create about themselves. As Liz Kleinrock shares in *Start Here, Start Now: A Guide to Antibias and Antiracist Work in Your School Community* (2021),

> If you're asking students to be vulnerable with you and their classmates, it's important to remember that trust and respect go both ways. I strongly believe that educators have to work consistently to humanize themselves to their students, and must view themselves as partners, not leaders, in this work. Modeling how to brainstorm ideas for this poem is an effective way for me to share aspects of my childhood, interests, and personal experiences. (10)

Figures 3.1 and 3.2 show the poem I wrote when I participated in the IDEAS foundational course Anti-Racist School Practices to Support the Success of All Students, followed by my son Cairo's poem that he wrote in middle school.

There are multiple learning benefits that come from engaging students in this activity. Students will need to *remember* and *understand* various aspects of their own lives and what Lyon has shared in her poem, *apply* that understanding as they *analyze* and *evaluate* Lyon's poem, and then use that analysis and evaluation to *create* their own. They will also develop a deeper understanding of key ideas and details, craft, and structure as well as have experience with integrating knowledge and ideas—all key components in most reading standards.

FIGURE 3.1   "Where I'm From" by Afrika Afeni Mills

## Where I'm From

I am from jazzy Harlem legacies

I am from *Mama's baby, go to sleep*

*Slide on down a dream . . .*

I am from watching quietly and wondering why

I am from loving Christmas to

Watching Christmas fade away

And then return.

I am from purple hymnals, sabbath keeping and cleaning out the leavening

I am from secret-keeping exploding into truth-telling and legalism transformed into

Deep intimacy with God

I am from most of my siblings

Gone too soon.

I am from feeling lonely in a crowd,

And then learning that I'm more seen than I

Ever imagined.

---

This activity will also help students to see how they can share important aspects of who they are, learn how to see beyond their perceptions of their classmates, and build on those skills to do the same with people outside of their home and learning communities all while continuing to develop their literacy skills.

In addition to sharing your own "Where I'm From" poem, you can provide students with examples of others. Lyon and Julie Landsman created the *I Am From Project*, and at the IAmFromProject.com website you can find dozens of sample poems to read, compare, contrast, and learn from.

As you brainstorm what students can include in their own "Where I'm From" poems, you can list the following potential ideas:

- Places you've lived

- Music your family enjoys

FIGURE 3.2 "Where I'm From" by Cairo Mills

## Where I'm From

I am from deep roots of family

from hanging out on weekends with my mom, dad,

sister, and a dog named Rabbit

I am from intelligence, respect, obedience, and love

I am from pine trees in my backyard

whose limbs guided me up to see a world anew

I am from action figures and video games

from Russell's and Mills's

I am from yelling and loving

and from having a big dinner when the family is together

from helping my grandma cook

I am from going to church every Sunday with my family

I am from the air force and even Ireland

from lemon pound cake and gumbo

from armies of war

and from segregation and racism

I am from Camp Mattatuck

I am from those moments where I can appreciate

what I have

I am from thanking those who gave me what I have

- Holidays your family celebrates

- Family traditions

- Relationships with different family members

- Sensory details that remind you of home: smells, tastes, sounds

In doing this work with students as an ABAR instructional practice, it's important to be intentional about noticing how race does and doesn't show up in "Where I'm From" poems. In comparing and contrasting my poem with my son's, Cairo names race explicitly ("I am from segregation and racism"), whereas a reader could infer it in mine ("I am from jazzy Harlem legacies"). If you notice that you have not included anything about your race, culture, or ethnicity in the *Where I'm From* poem you model for your class, I recommend adding it to your poem to open the door for students to do the same.

Figures 3.3 and 3.4 show examples from siblings Gaby and Sebastian; isn't it interesting to see how children from the same family background celebrate different aspects of their identities?

FIGURE 3.3  "I Am Poem" by Gaby (Fifth Grade)

---

### I Am Poem

I am an athlete, a cook, and a reader.

I am not disrespectful.

I come from Massachusetts.

I dream of new discoveries.

I fear pigeons.

I hope to be an archeologist.

I love family, friends, and animals.

\*\*\*\*\*\*

Objects sacred to me:

Object #1: a book. I chose a book because I love reading. Reading is one of my favorite things to do.

—Sentence 1 in I am poem.

Object #2: my stuffed pig (pinkie). I chose pinkie because she shows my love for animals, how i like to sleep a lot, and it also shows a piece of me that has been with me forever.

—Sentence 7 in I am poem

Object #3: my piano. I chose my piano because it shows my love for music. It also shows how I like to try new things and how I am very creative.

—Sentence 4 in I am poem.

I think that this journey makes me feel happy and patient. I think this because I took the time to find sacred objects and to think of fun memories and enjoyable moments in my past.

---

FIGURE 3.4  "I Am Poem" by Sebastian (Grade 7)

## I Am Poem

**I am**

A son

An older brother

A dog owner

A soccer player

Colombian

Venezuelan

Respectful

Impatient

From seeing family

From a family of dentists

Someone who doesn't want to be a dentist

**I am Not**

Boring

Disrespectful

An actor

A liar (I couldn't be even if I wanted to)

**I Came from**

Colombia and Venezuela

Early-in-the-morning Brookline Rec soccer games

**I Dream**

One day there will be no more climate change

No more hatred

That 80,000 people will be cheering my name when I score the game winning goal

in the World Cup

**I fear**

Some problems, it is to solve them

My parents will get COVID-19

My grandma will get COVID-19, and not make it through

**I Hope**

To live a life of no regret

For the COVID-19 pandemic to be over

To go more days to school

For no more mask wearing

**I love**

My family

My *true* friends

Soccer

Colombia

Venezuela

Home

School (in person school)

Going to Stowe

Visiting family

Vacation

## CREATING "I AM" POSTERS/PRESENTATIONS

Several years ago, in preparation for connecting with the participants in a workshop and modeling ways to build relationships and community with students, I created a digital poster that reflected some of the important parts of who I am—the things and people that make me Afrika. My "I Am" poster (shown in Figure 3.5) included pictures of things like the following:

- Me, my husband, and our two children

- Me and my husband dancing at a wedding

- Me and my siblings when I was younger

- The birthday cake my mom made for my fortieth birthday

- My son playing soccer

- My daughter playing the flute

- My wedding invitation

FIGURE 3.5  Afrika's "I Am" poster

My choice to share specific images and memories revealed things about me to those who viewed my poster. What viewers can infer is that I value being married, being a mom, spending time together with my family, having celebrations, and being playful. You can engage your students in this activity as well.

Provide students with the opportunity to create a similar poster or presentation that explores the different parts of who they are by engaging in each of the following steps:

- Form agreements as a class regarding what types of images should and should not be included in an identity poster/presentation, and discuss the rationale for the agreement (e.g., *We want all images and words to inform, celebrate, and uplift, and not to offend or cause harm.*).

- Ask students to identify important people in their lives, favorite places to visit, special occasions and celebrations, books and movies they enjoy, hobbies, things they like to eat, and things that make them smile.

- Students gather images representing those things from Internet searches, photos from their phones and families, and/or from creating their own images through drawing and painting. (This would be a great opportunity to collaborate with the art/media teacher.)

- Guide students to decide which images to include in a final version.

- Students create a digital poster, slideshow, and/or audio/video recording capturing the selected images.

- Invite students to share and discuss their posters/presentations with their classmates using a Gallery Walk or similar protocol that allows students to share impressions, questions, and connections with one another.

The learning benefits of this activity include building comprehension and collaboration skills as well as their ability to present their knowledge and ideas that are part of most speaking and listening standards. All students need to learn how to effectively develop the organization, style, and purpose of a presentation in order to convey a message that is appropriate for their audience, and to use digital media to deepen the audience's understanding of the content.

As with the "Where I'm From" poem, it's important that you create your own as a model for students and talk with them about why you chose the images you included. Similarly, notice where race does and doesn't show up in the "I Am" poster/presentation. It may be a bit easier to notice with the images in the presentations than with the words in a poem, yet still important to name so that the impact of race on our identity transitions from implicit to explicit. This is particularly important for White students in predominantly White communities who likely have grown up surrounded by people who also identify as White and images of Whiteness in the media and in the curriculum. This can cause them to think of Whiteness as "normal." If everyone in a student's presentation is the same race, this can be an opportunity to open a window for them and ask "Who is missing from your story, and why are they missing?"

# Breathe and Reflect

Try writing your own "Where I'm From" poem or creating your own "I Am" poster. How did you decide what to include? What were the challenges? How did writing/ creating prepare you to support students as they did the same? What are some things you would have included in your poem or on your poster when you were the age of your current students? ■

_____

_____

_____

_____

_____

_____

_____

_____

_____

_____

_____

_____

_____

_____

_____

_____

_____

_____

_____

_____

_____

_____

_____

_____

_____

## Sharing Name Stories to Understand Identity

My name is Afrika. Not Africa. Not af-REE-kah like paprika. Afrika like the continent. Not the country. The continent. And Afeni. Not ah-FEE-NEE. Ah-FAY-nee after Afeni Shakur of the Black Panther Party. Afeni like Tupac's mom. As an adult, my name is one of my favorite parts of who I am, but when I was in elementary school, I didn't really like my name. I went to school with mostly Black students and, unfortunately, internalized oppression manifested as anti-Black sentiments and espousing misinformation about Africa and led some of my classmates to make fun of my name. Tired of being teased one day, I remember telling a new friend that my name was Andrea— kind of like what actress Uzo Aduba experienced when she asked her mom to call her Zoe instead of Uzoamaka when she was a child because her classmates and teachers struggled to pronounce her name. Uzo's mom declined and said that if her classmates and teachers could learn to say Dostoyevsky and Tchaikovsky, they could learn to say Uzoamaka.

https://bit.ly/3v6ZaY2

What if Uzo's teachers had partnered with her mom to give that message to Uzo as well? What if my teachers let my classmates know that it wasn't okay to make fun of my name? I don't remember my teachers intervening when I was teased. In fact, my gym teacher, though he probably meant it as a joke, would call me every other continent when I came to his class. Looking back, I don't think having him call me North America and Asia sent the message to my classmates that my name was special and to be respected.

When I wasn't being teased, I grew tired of people regularly misspelling my name, even though I understood why it happened. How cool would it have been in elementary school if instead of focusing on Eurocentric content like reading Shakespeare and learning Latin we also learned accurate content about the African continent? That's not to say I wouldn't have been teased, but I can't help but wonder if I would have felt a greater affinity for my name at a younger age.

Creating space for your students to reflect on and share their name stories is a powerful way to begin to build from curiosity and awareness about themselves to curiosity and awareness about others.

### EXPLORING THE POWER OF NAMES THROUGH INTERACTIVE READ ALOUDS

Thankfully there are many educators who are engaging students in an ABAR approach to interactive read alouds. Sarah Halter Hahesy (she/her/hers) is a third-grade teacher with Brookline Public Schools in Massachusetts, a district that is a mix of urban and suburban. Sarah has created a small group of peers at her school who meet monthly to discuss their antiracist teaching. Sarah has shared the following unit plan as an example of how to explore the power of names using interactive read alouds.

In the unit plan, Sarah identifies the following:

- The book titles and authors

- The purpose of using the books as interactive read alouds (these books support the discussion of the importance of people knowing and correctly pronouncing names and feature characters from racial groups who are not always included as mentor texts)

- The big idea/focus questions for the interactive read alouds (in this unit, the focus questions are *Is a name just a word or something more?* and *Why are names important?*)

- Teaching moves for before, during, and after reading (such as think-pair-share, think-pair-write/draw, turn and talk, or stop and jot).

Sarah explores the importance of names with students using four picture books. And picture books are effective with students of all ages because of their brevity, color, and clear language. The unit plan includes stopping points throughout the books with questions and teaching moves (i.e., turn and talk) to help build student comprehension:

*My Name Is Maria Isabel* by Alma Flor Ada

Sample question during reading:

- What advice would you give Maria Isabel about how to fix the problem with her being called the wrong name?

*The Name Jar* by Yansook Choi

Sample question during reading:

- How did her classmates decide to help Unhei find her name?

*Thunder Boy Jr.* by Sherman Alexie

Sample question during reading:

- Why would someone want a "normal" name?

*Alma and How She Got Her Name* by Juana Martinez-Neal

Sample question during reading:

- Alma has six names. How many names do you have?

After reading, Sarah wraps up each lesson by reflecting on the big ideas of the book and planning what she will say to guide students to pull their ideas together to support the big idea (e.g., *What story do you want your name to tell the world?*). The unit culminates with Sarah partnering with families to support students as they engage in recording their own name stories. Some of the questions students ask their families include the following:

- Does my name have a special meaning? If so, what does it mean?

- Who chose my name? Why was it chosen?

- Do I have any nicknames? How were they given?

- A fun fact I learned about my name when talking with my family was . . .

In her book *Rebellious Read Alouds*, Vera Ahiyya (2022) offers ready-to-go interactive read aloud lessons centered on specific books by and about people from traditionally marginalized groups. Vera's Instagram accounts, @thetututeacher and @diversereads, offer daily and weekly suggestions for new books to share with young students. Remember, picture books work for students of all ages!

Students then share their name stories in a circle if they're meeting in person, or using Flipgrid (https://info.flipgrid.com/) if they're meeting virtually. The purpose of the share is for students to get to know one another better and to build a sense of identity and belonging.

## A Note About Banned Books

In Chapter 4, we will explore how to navigate resistance to ABAR instructional practices, but it's important to specifically note here that resistance to books by and about people from marginalized groups is increasing, with several headline-grabbing instances during the time I wrote this book. If you are facing book bans or challenges in your district, it will be important for you to have a foundational understanding of critical race theory, to be able to speak to the difference between indoctrination and education, and know the purpose and benefits of your instructional decisions. It'll be important to talk with your administrator(s) about your plans so they can proactively plan to support you and your students by planning a response to potential pushback from families and/or the community, advocating for your students with the school board/committee, securing funding for book and curricular purchases and for related professional learning experiences, and also providing and protecting time to collaborate with colleagues.

## EXPLORING THE POWER OF NAMES
## THROUGH LITERATURE STUDY

Literature studies—in which students have the opportunity to examine literary devices, elements, and structures in poetry and narrative fiction like plot, conflict, setting, similes, metaphors, allusion, point of view, and theme—provide occasions for students to connect with authors and characters through name exploration. Names play an important role in many of the novels students read, whether independently or as whole-class readings. You can use literature studies to guide students into deeper study about the power of names in characters—what does the name mean? Is it symbolic in any way? What images come to mind when you read, say, or hear this name? You can then move the discussion into more personal reflection on the power of students' names.

Megan Mathes (she/her) has been teaching high school English in independent schools in Florida, New York, and Oregon for the past twenty-three years. Megan embeds name and identity exploration with her students using mentor texts like "My Name" by Sandra Cisneros (1991) where they consider the following:

- What does your name mean?

- Do you know why your name was chosen?

- Do you have a nickname? How did you get it? How do you feel about it?

- Do you have a middle name?

- Has anyone ever commented on your name? If so, what did they say, and how did the comment make you feel?

- Do you think your name causes people to treat you in a particular way? How? Share an example.

- Have you considered changing your name? If so, why? What would you change it to?

In order to effectively support your students as they engage in an exploration of their own name stories, you will need to prepare by answering these questions about your name, and to share your answers with your students. Figures 3.6 and 3.7 provide examples that two of Megan's sophomore students wrote in response.

Brigitte has captured so much here about her name. In it, the reader can see that she knows the meaning of her name and the historical and cultural connection it has for her to the point where she can beautifully depict it as an experience in a Parisian café sixty years ago. Brigitte also recognizes the relationship and struggle that others have had with her name, how people have misperceived or avoided her name, yet her connection to her name has remained strong.

FIGURE 3.6  Brigitte's Name Story

## The Story of My Name

Brigitte,

It's a mouthful to look at and a handful to say.

It is intimidating.

As if it is the Mount Everest of names.

They either make the attempt of stumbling through it,

or they make no attempt at all.

Instead they ask, "How do you say it?" "Could you remind me?" "Where is it from?" There is a third option too.

It is one where they are too afraid to even look at it.

Instead, they pretend it is just a normal "American" name.

Whey they say it out loud, it becomes plain, generic.

It loses a syllable too; there is an E at the end of it for a reason.

It wasn't put there just to make it look pretty.

It transforms into a stern word.

One that sounds like I am in trouble or have done something wrong. It becomes short but not sweet,

just how they like it,

and of course easy to speak.

It loses its grammar, its history, its purpose.

In its mother tongue, it is graceful, elegant, and has a slight je ne sais quoi that accompanies it wherever it is sung.

When I hear it out loud, it reminds me of an old forgotten song that lives on in my heart, one that drifts through the air as I look out my window into the night.

How does it sound? you ask. Well let me show you,

You are in Paris, it is summer, sometime in the 1960s. You look around and find yourself sitting outside at your favorite local café about to finish your dinner, don't worry, it's not one of the touristy ones, in fact, it is anything but. As it grows late, the street begins to quiet, and time seems to slow, you can feel the heat of the night encompass you like a warm embrace while you slowly sip on your nightcap, carefully watching the jazz trio that performs on the street corner. As you leave and begin to walk home for the night, the maître d' calls out "bonne soirée Brigitte."

He says the name as though it is a small boat rolling over the waves of a stormy sea, bobbing up and down with each syllable.

It sounds like home, a home I have not visited in awhile, but home nonetheless. My name means strength, power, vigor, and virtue,

but it can also mean that you are a little stubborn.

It means that you believe in yourself, in all parts of yourself, even when you are out of tune. But don't worry, as soon as you hear its song drifting through the warm summer's breeze, you will once more believe.

Brynn's name story (see Figure 3.7) provides a great example of not only exploring the cultural, historical, and familial significance of her name but also what it means to struggle with wanting to fit in. The online companion contains links to more resources you can use with students that contain mentor texts and support the exploration of name meanings (resources.corwin.com/openwindows).

FIGURE 3.7  Brynn's Name Story

### Underneath the Letters

It's fascinating how a name can be so brief and short but hold so much internal depth and meaning. Brynn! It seems so simple with just one vowel, ever so delicate and pretty. But what is truly underneath those five letters?

My name, Brynn, is a direct link to my heritage and family. The name is a Welsh male name, traditionally spelled with just one *n*. It means *little hill* in Welsh, depicting the landscape of the small country. My mother's family originated from Cardiff, Wales, with both of my grandparents being born and raised there. Welsh culture is very special to my family, carrying on the traditions brought down from generation to generation. When my parents were thinking of what to name their first daughter, they immediately knew they wanted a Welsh name.

To me, having an unusual "foreign" name hasn't always been easy. I truly do value the direct link that it has to my heritage. I cherish how my name is a testament to all the different backgrounds I have that aren't also portrayed on the outside. It's like a window for others to look into my family's culture without opening the entire door.

At times though, I wished that my name was just as simple and known as my parents and siblings: Jack, Ryan, Emma, John, and David. All have significant meaning but don't stand out. Whenever someone would butcher the pronunciation of my name, a sense of embarrassment filled within, like it was my fault someone couldn't carefully read letters. I would frown that my name would immediately make me different from everyone else and was the only one nobody could ever say or spell correctly. I craved to have a more generic name.

As I grew older, the shame that used to drown my confidence slowly turned to pride. Brynn was the name a strong, fierce Welsh rugby player would have. The type of player that was driven and resilient. The player that was unstoppable. I was born to be the toughest, most powerful girl, Brynn! I was born to be the person the name was always intended for. My name was meant to inspire me. To always demonstrate kindness and warmth like the petals of a flower but to also have the strength of the stem supporting me along the way. Once I learned what was exactly below the surface of each letter, *b, r, y, n, n*, I understood the direct connection it had to the person I am. Being sweet and kind on the outside but tough and driven on the inside.

# Breathe and Reflect

What is your name story? How do you feel about your name? Use this space to tell the story of what your name means to you. What have you noticed about your students' relationships with their names? ■

_____

_____

_____

_____

_____

_____

_____

_____

_____

_____

_____

_____

_____

_____

_____

_____

_____

_____

_____

_____

_____

_____

_____

_____

_____

## HELPING STUDENTS UNDERSTAND THE COMPLEXITY OF IDENTITY

Identity is so complex! As I was growing up and my parents shared stories with me about my ancestors and Black History, I wondered about some things. Although I knew, for example, that I was a descendant of Africans who were enslaved, I also noticed that my hair length, texture, and skin tone differed from other people who also identified as Black, and I noticed that there seemed to be both positive and negative feelings connected to phrases I would hear about being *light-skinned* and having *good hair*.

That curiosity never left me, so when, a couple of years ago, I had the opportunity to learn more about my heritage through AncestryDNA, I had even more questions. What does it mean, for example, that 30% of my DNA traces back to European countries? I believe my great-grandfather, John Bass, on my mom's side was either biracial or White based on census records I found through AncestryDNA. Does that part of my DNA come from him—a man who I hear loved my Black great-grandmother, Carrie Moore, and who created a family with her in Virginia prior to the *Loving v. Virginia* ruling that struck down anti-miscegenation laws in 1967? Or does it come from something more sinister tracing back to the violence that many enslaved women experienced? Is it both? I may not ever have answers to these questions, but I can affirm my identity by exploring the different aspects of who I am that are known to me.

https://bit.ly/3OoKpYa

As an educator, you can build on the learning experiences of students writing "Where I'm From" poems, creating "I Am" identity presentations, and reflecting on the power of their names to create space for students to learn more about the complex, expansive nature of our identities, similar to what I experienced when I reflected on my AncestryDNA results. For middle and secondary students, in particular, a resource like "Identity & Community: An Introduction to 6th Grade Social Studies" unit from Facing History & Ourselves provides learning experiences that help students to learn more deeply about themselves and others. Each of the lessons includes an introduction (overview, learning goals, and materials) and the lesson plan (warm-up, main activity, follow-through, homework, and curricular connections); students explore critical questions like the following:

- *Who am I?*

- *What shapes my identity?*

- *How do others define their identities?*

- *What aspects of our identity do we show to others?*

- *What is community?*

- *How do communities define* we *and* they?

- *What does it mean to belong?*

We are composed of our social identifiers: where we grew up; our position in/relationship with our families; our school experiences; our beliefs; our personalities and preferences; sense of humor; the people/things we love; important memories; what makes us laugh, feel peace, and a sense of belonging; our fears, triggers, and pet peeves; and our accomplishments as well as our hopes, dreams, and wishes. You can help students to identify how all facets of their identity interact to make them unique. The activities here can be especially useful in finding links of empathy between individuals and groups. Once students have the opportunity to answer these questions about themselves, their families, and their communities, they will be better equipped to gaze through windows to see how people who are racially different answer these questions.

## WHITE IDENTITY DEVELOPMENT AND IDENTIFYING AS AN ANTIRACIST

When we consider resistance to antiracist instructional practices, we recognize that some people fear that their White-identifying children will be made to feel bad for being White. Engaging in race-related discussions with students, when done well, should never be about shame and guilt. Teachers can use these questions with students to help them to see that they have choices when it comes to White identity. Being White does not have to mean being a colonizer or oppressor. Being White can mean working as part of a larger human family to make sure that everyone has access to what they need to live whole, joyful lives—this includes the way we see and talk about other people, what we believe about them, questioning where those beliefs come from, the way we vote, the neighborhoods we choose to live in, speaking up in the face of unfairness, whose voices we listen to and elevate, the questions we ask, and our openness to shifting our thoughts and beliefs when we encounter new information.

https://bit.ly/3Otb4Df

Deepening this understanding can look, for example, like reading *She Stood for Freedom: The Untold Story of a Civil Rights Hero, Joan Trumpauer Mulholland* (Mulholland 2016) with students or watching and discussing the documentary called *An Ordinary Hero: The True Story of Joan Trumpauer Mulholland* (Mulholland

2013) and reflecting on those learnings using tools like what Elizabeth Denevi and Lori Cohen (2020), collaborating as part of the Eastern Educational Resource Collaborative, shared in the "White Antiracist Activist" resource on the *Teaching While White* blog. This list captures the stories of people who identify as White who were/are also ABAR activists. In addition to White students benefiting from the opportunity to gaze through windows to learn about people who are racially different, they can also learn about people who identify the same racially and took a stand as abolitionists, resisters, and those who committed to working in solidarity with Black, Indigenous, and People of Color (BIPOC). The resource encourages teachers to support students as they learn about these activists with some of the following questions:

1. In considering the activists' lives, what were the significant moments that led to their activism? What motivated them to work for change?

2. What skills do/did they need to challenge racial injustice?

3. What blind spots might these activists have?

4. How can White people work effectively in solidarity with People of Color? How do they keep from replicating the very system they are trying to challenge?

5. What is the value of a multiracial, antiracist coalition?

6. What actions might you take to work for racial justice?

## Breathe and Reflect

If your students identify as White, reflect on how these antiracist examples can expand how they think about what their racial identity means? Which White antiracist activist might you explore with your students from the Teaching While White resource? ▪

_____

_____

_____

_____

_____

_____

_____

_____

_____

_____

_____

_____

_____

_____

_____

_____

_____

_____

_____

_____

_____

_____

_____

_____

_____

_____

_____

_____

If students can, through the experiences outlined in this chapter, develop an age-appropriate understanding of themselves and others, they will be better equipped to navigate through the stages of racial awareness as they enter adulthood. As part of their ABAR K–12 experiences, students can challenge the color-blind perspective of the contact stage, avoid the feelings of guilt and shame that come with the disintegration stage, and counter the misperceptions of the reintegration stage. Instead, they'll be able to experience the positive racial identification of the pseudo-independence stage, connect with others who both share their racial identity and identify as antiracists indicated at the immersion/emersion stage, and have the strong foundation needed to connect positive racial identity with what it means to actively pursue social justice and antiracist beliefs and practices.

# CHAPTER 4

# Navigating Resistance and Creating Brave Classroom Spaces

There are seasons in this work of becoming and being an antibias, antiracist (ABAR) practitioner. In the fall, leaves die to make room for new growth. In the winter, root systems are growing underground, even though we can't see them. In the spring, we begin to witness new growth budding from that root system. In the summer, we begin to enjoy the fruit of what has grown. This chapter focuses on what it is like to be in the autumn and winter of this work where we go through stages of grief as old practices die, new practices begin to take root, and the growth, though critical, can be hard to see.

Now that you and your students have explored and developed your own racial identities, this chapter will help you to navigate the external and internal resistance you are likely to experience as you shift to ABAR instructional practices. Resistance can come in many forms, such as an e-mail or a Facebook post from a parent, or a student who doesn't want to participate, or colleagues who aren't yet on the same ABAR journey. And resistance can come from within us; this is hard work that requires unlearning and relearning, having difficult conversations, and overcoming societal and systemic norms. When we reflect on what ABAR practitioners have shared about their own educational experiences in Chapter 1—what they experienced, what they wish had been different—it can inspire us to be different in our own instructional practices. Inspiration, however, can only last but so long if we aren't honest about what truly scares us about changing our mindsets and instructional practices. As James Baldwin stated, "Not everything that is faced can be changed, but nothing can be changed until it is faced" (Baldwin 1962).

In order to be prepared for the challenges that come with this work, let's take a deeper dive into four typical challenges that educators face with ABAR instruction:

- Lack of experience with race-based conversations

- Lack of coursework about race in teacher prep programs

- Fear of pushback by administrators, families, and/or the school board

- Lack of instructional materials for race-based conversations

## LACK OF EXPERIENCE WITH RACE-BASED CONVERSATIONS

Teachers didn't grow up learning how to have conversations about race or exploring racial inequities. In her 2017 TEDx Talk "Is My Skin Brown Because I Drank Chocolate Milk?" Beverly Daniel Tatum (2017a) encourages listeners to take a moment to think about their earliest race-related memory and what emotion is attached to that memory. The related memories for many are from kindergarten and stir confusion, anxiety, fear, embarrassment, sadness, and shame. Tatum also asks if they discussed this experience when it occurred with a parent, teacher, or another caring adult. The group of Stanford first-year students she asked commented that they didn't share it with anyone, which Tatum notes is peculiar because most five-to-seven-year-olds are pretty candid and don't filter themselves. She wondered if they had already been shushed or learned that they're not supposed to talk about race (Tatum 2017a).

Even if we didn't grow up with the opportunity to discuss what we noticed about racial differences and difficult societal issues when we were young, we can learn how to do it now. Just like we learn how to do other challenging things (e.g., differentiate instruction, support students' development of mathematical reasoning, teach literary analysis), we can learn how to do this challenging thing. Just like we encourage students to shift from a fixed mindset to a growth mindset as they're engaging in new learning experiences, we can shift to a growth mindset about ourselves as diverse, equitable, inclusive, culturally responsive ABAR practitioners.

https://bit.ly/3v5sZls

There are very helpful, free resources that can support us as we engage in this work, like Learning for Justice's (n.d.) *Let's Talk!: Facilitating Critical Conversations With Students*, which we'll explore later in the chapter; many are listed and cited throughout this book. The online companion contains an extensive link library to get you started (resources.corwin.com/openwindows).

## Breathe and Reflect

What is something challenging that, with effort, you learned to do (e.g., a new language, instrument, sport, undergraduate/graduate studies, new standards, curriculum)? How did you get better at it? How is ABAR work with students different from other hard things you've learned to do? What is at risk if you don't engage in this work? ▪

_____

_____

_____

_____

_____

_____

_____

_____

_____

_____

_____

_____

_____

_____

_____

_____

_____

_____

_____

_____

_____

_____

_____

# LACK OF COURSEWORK ABOUT
# RACE IN TEACHER PREP PROGRAMS

In a study conducted by EdWeek Research Center in 2020, only 18% of educators said they received antiracist/abolitionist training in their educator preparation programs, with just 30% saying that they received such professional development in their districts or schools. In my educator prep program, I learned about the history of education in the United States, the impact the Individuals with Disabilities Education Act should have on my instructional practices, and how to teach reading and math. While it was fun and refreshing to learn how to use manipulatives in math instruction (a very different experience than how I learned about math), and the importance of phonemic awareness, there's a lot more I needed to learn.

Although many of us didn't have these experiences as part of our educator preparation programs, we can engage in that learning now.

Just as we create space to take deep dives into new standards, new math, literacy, history, and science curricula, we can create spaces and time to learn how to engage students in fuller learning experiences when it comes to race. We mustn't try to do this work alone. We can create teams to engage in socially just, inclusive, accurate curriculum development. That way, when a textbook refers to enslaved Africans as "workers" and "immigrants," we have a space where we can challenge this false narrative. (The online companion provides a list of links to articles and online resources to help you with this work, resources.corwin.com/openwindows.)

Here are a few resources that can support you as you engage in antiracist learning (these and other resources are linked in the online companion to this book):

- "All Students Need Anti-Racism Education" | Christina Torres | Learning for Justice

  https://bit.ly/3v26V20

- "An Open Letter to a Parent Afraid of Anti-Racist Education" | Christina Torres | EducationWeek

  https://bit.ly/3lhDpJp

- "Anti-Racist Work in Schools: Are You in It for the Long Haul?" | Elizabeth Kleinrock | Learning for Justice

  https://bit.ly/3Hb3Uih

- "Finding the Courage to Be Specific About Systemic Racism in Education" | Matthew Kay | ASCD

  https://bit.ly/3JOquin

- "How I Learned to Stop Worrying and Love Discussing Race" | Jay Smooth | TEDx

  https://bit.ly/3Hhf8l6

- "Shifting Out of Neutral" | Jonathan Gold | Learning for Justice

  https://bit.ly/3hdcMt3

- "Students Say Teach the Truth" | Elizabeth Kleinrock | Learning for Justice

  https://bit.ly/3vfXr38

- "Unpacking 'I'm Afraid': Confronting Colleagues Who Avoid Teaching & Talking About Race" | Reanna Ursin | Teaching While White

  https://bit.ly/3BPKgXL

# Breathe and Reflect

What coursework did you engage in in your educator preparation programs where you learned how to have conversations with students about race or explore racial inequities? If you didn't have this experience, what would you like to have learned to prepare you for these conversations? ■

_____

_____

_____

_____

_____

_____

_____

_____

_____

_____

_____

_____

_____

_____

_____

_____

_____

_____

_____

_____

_____

_____

_____

_____

_____

# Fear of Pushback by Administrators, Families, and/or the School Board

This is a big one. There's a good chance that engaging in ABAR instructional practices will provoke questions and concerns from administrators, families, and/or community members. In fact, as I write this chapter, we're seeing a lot of this resistance showing up in communities around the United States. This content may be unfamiliar and bring into question some long-standing beliefs and false impressions about people who are racially different. Sometimes we see resistance from families when teachers let students know about the problematic past of authors like Dr. Seuss, shift to focusing on learning about Indigenous People while telling the truth about Columbus, or decenter White authors to amplify the writings of Black, Indigenous, and People of Color (BIPOC). At the heart of pushback from White families when it comes to engaging in this learning is the concern that when White students begin to learn about the history of colonization and oppression of BIPOC, not only in the United States but around the world, they will develop a sense of shame and guilt about being White. And yes, this is a possibility if this learning is not facilitated skillfully. However, the tools throughout this book can help teachers to facilitate ABAR learning in a way that is student centered, wholehearted, and identity affirming.

Although some concerns about pushback may feel like barriers, they could help us to grapple with considerations that can inform things we may not see. Additionally, providing White students with clearer mirrors—or, showing them examples of White ABAR advocates—can help us to create learning experiences and environments that help White students to make the connection to people who look like them who engaged in liberatory work. While there are White people who have used, are using, and will use their privilege and advantages to oppress, there are also White people who have used and will use their privilege and advantages to freedom dream alongside the marginalized, as Bettina Love (2019) discusses in *We Want to Do More Than Survive*, because they realize that their liberation is bound up with those who are oppressed. White students and their families need to know that they have a choice concerning what Whiteness can be and that, in your classroom, they will learn about what it means to become a good ancestor, as Layla Saad (2020) discusses in *Me and White Supremacy*.

## PARTNERING WITH FAMILIES

Many of us have heard the saying "I'd rather ask for forgiveness than for permission." This approach is understandable. When our awareness is awakened, we don't want there to be any interruption to the work we want to do with our students to create a more inclusive and equitable learning community. When we move forward without attempting to partner with families, however, we not only miss out on the opportunity to potentially partner with those who can be advocates, supporters, and allies in this work but we also don't provide families with the opportunities to ask important questions.

Figure 4.1 shows an example of a letter that second-grade teacher Kara Pranikoff wrote to the families of her students in response to the Derek Chauvin trial. Kara communicates with families regularly about the conversations that take place in her classroom, sharing the context for the conversation, pointing out the questions students asked and the responses some made, and listing the books or articles the class reads and responds to together. In this way, Kara shows partnership with the families of the children in her care and opens a door for communication.

**FIGURE 4.1    Family Letter From Kara Pranikoff Regarding the Derek Chauvin Trial**

---

April 22, 2021

Dear Families,

We gathered in school yesterday and, is often the case, a time to talk about *World Events* was listed on our schedule. As the students came in and started their morning routine of unpacking and getting ready for the day a few students gathered close. They came in with their own information having witnessed their parents attentive to the news, like the rest of the country, waiting for the verdict in the trial of Derek Chauvin. They understood that our classroom was a place where we would be talking about the events that the larger community was processing.

Our classroom discussion took the same shape as many others which have unfolded this year. We worked from the information that the students already know. We clarify facts. We grapple with questions. We connect to other pieces of learning we've had across our time together.

In this instance, all the students remembered the protests which erupted in response to the murder of George Floyd. They recalled conversations in their first grade classrooms about what had happened and, for many, their first memories of the Black Lives Matter Movement which has been a running part of our classroom conversations this year. As is always the case, they asked some large questions about the underlying issues that the Chauvin case unearths: racism, prejudice, excessive police force, steps we can take towards a more equitable future.

Here are some of the comments and questions that students shared across both cohorts:

- Why didn't people help George Floyd?

- This is not the only person with Black skin to be killed by police.

- How long will he be in jail?

- What can we do instead of jail?

- When did Racism start?

---

- It's not really happy. There are a lot of emotions.

- No one should be killed.

- Police do not often get in trouble.

- Why didn't the other police officers speak up?

- There was a video so no one could lie about what happened.

- Will it get better?

These conversations are the bedrock of making change. The only way to shift the cycle of systemic racism in our country is through education and open discussion. In fact, as the conversation closed, a few students asked if they could write about what was on their minds or make signs to declare their thoughts.

I was reminded of these actions of our second graders in the evening as I read Dr. Esau McCaulley's powerful opinion piece in the *New York Times*—"My children and the students committed to my care have to live in this world and be frustrated by it, but they do not have to accept it as unchangeable. They do not have to give way to apathy. They are free to weep and mourn as long as they need to do so, but they can also resist. They can plan, organize, protest and march." (see https://nyti.ms/3v51hMm)

These conversations in school, in your homes, throughout our community are never easy, but they do leave me hopeful. Raising children who have clarity about our country's history and a vision for how we can do better is our greatest hope. If you are looking for some additional resources to guide your own thinking, there are some excellent resources embedded in this article from the Minnesota Public Radio (see https://bit.ly/3JCL8lh).

As always, please reach out with any questions. It has been a year full of difficult conversations. A year like none other. I am continually grateful to teach in a school and a community who is working toward systemic change.

In solidarity,

Kara

---

There are many helpful resources to support partnering with families from organizations such as Learning for Justice and Teaching While White; I've provided links in the online companion: resources.corwin.com/openwindows.

# Breathe and Reflect

How have you experienced (or anticipated) pushback from your administration, students' families, and/or the larger school community if you've engaged in conversations about race or exploring racial inequities with your students? ■

_____

_____

_____

_____

_____

_____

_____

_____

_____

_____

_____

_____

_____

_____

_____

_____

_____

_____

_____

_____

_____

_____

_____

_____

_____

_____

_____

_____

_____

# Lack of Instructional Materials for Race-Based Conversations

In the same EdWeek Research Center (2020) study, 84% of educators indicated that they are at least somewhat willing to teach or support the implementation of an antiracist curriculum, but only 14% say that they have both the professional development training and resources to do so. This is something I can relate to. After spending two years on maternity leave early in my teaching career, I accepted a position teaching fourth grade in a brand-new community-based school that was terribly underresourced. Unfortunately, because of tensions between the community members who advocated for the creation of the school and the school department, tens of thousands of dollars in instructional supplies funding was reabsorbed into the district budget, and we started the year in this brand-new, state-of-the-art building with no instructional materials. We had a dance studio and an art room with a pottery kiln but no books, paper, pencils, crayons, or markers. We only received the math curriculum to ensure that the school would be in alignment with the rest of the district in this one content area. That was a very challenging year, and I relied heavily on the library and Scholastic Book Fair points for free books. Budgetary constraints are very real considerations, but I've found that there are ways to identify and implement free, high-quality instructional resources.

For example:

- Facing History & Ourselves has units of study, teaching strategies, and classroom materials.

- Learning for Justice has standards, lessons, learning plans, teaching strategies, student tasks and rubrics, and a library of student texts.

- The Strategic Education Research Partnership has interdisciplinary units of study for upper elementary and middle school students that include readers' theater, word study, and debate/discussion opportunities.

- The Zinn Education Project provides lessons, roleplays, and teaching guides and activities that you can sort by time period, theme, and resource type.

These resources can help educators create a fuller learning experience for students, and we'll explore them more in later chapters.

# Breathe and Reflect

Based on times you've had to be resourceful in the past, use this space to begin to create an action plan for finding and acquiring the resources you need to help you to engage students in conversations about race. ▪

_____

_____

_____

_____

_____

_____

_____

_____

_____

_____

_____

_____

_____

_____

_____

_____

_____

_____

_____

_____

_____

_____

_____

_____

# NAVIGATING RESISTANCE BY PARTNERING WITH COLLEAGUES

Because many teachers have not had coursework or practical experience navigating race in the classroom, it's helpful to collaborate in this work for a number of reasons. First, with a common goal, you and your colleagues create an allyship that can serve as a support network. You can share scenarios, role-play, or offer suggestions in response to specific situations. Second, you can set short-term and long-term goals for your ABAR journey as well as outcomes you'd like to see for your classroom and school community. And, third, you can hold one another accountable, gently nudging along the path, asking difficult questions, sharing resources, and responding to ideas.

https://bit.ly/37E1eOj

Lina Lopez-Ryan (she/her), Karen Sekiguchi (she/her), and Kerry Zagarella (she/her/they) work together as a team at the Winthrop School in Ipswich, Massachusetts. Lina is a Grade 3 teacher, Karen is the library/media specialist, and Kerry is a kindergarten teacher. In addition to establishing a social justice professional learning community at their school and creating the This School Is Your School website stating their pledge and mission, they developed the goals/action plan shown in Figure 4.2.

---

FIGURE 4.2  Goals/Action Plan Developed by Winthrop's Social Justice Professional Learning Community—Summer 2020

---

1. **Common Language**

   Within five years, our school community will have a common language and systems (practices, routines, sentence starters, etc.) to engage respectfully in productive and challenging conversations about social justice issues.

   - Research models and systems for having discussions on social justice issues.

   - Choose models to pilot in the classroom and with staff/peers.

   - Establish set of vocab, working definitions (akin to social thinking).

   - Display, post in classroom, actively publicize vocab.

   - Observing model teachers (videos, other schools, teachers in our schools) having conversations with students.

   - Establish common norms among staff and classroom re: accountable talk.

---

*(Continued)*

(Continued)

2. **Staff Development**

Within five years, our staff will have a unified commitment to antiracist teaching that is supported by ongoing training/professional development.

- Advocate for districtwide commitment to providing ongoing professional development on antiracist teaching.
- All staff and administration must participate in the professional development.
- Advocate and actively recruit a diverse staff (fellows, interviewing questions).
- Establish partnerships/collaborate with other communities with a commitment to antiracism work.
- Incorporate antiracist training through teacher-to-teacher mentoring.

3. **Curriculum and Teaching Practices**

Teachers will unpack and begin to implement social justice standards in order to create an inclusive curriculum that centers and amplifies diverse voices.

- Advocate for districtwide commitment to providing ongoing professional development on antiracist teaching.
- **All** staff and administration must participate in the professional development.
- Advocate for and actively recruit a diverse staff (including teaching fellows) and develop relevant interview questions.
- Establish partnerships/collaborate with other communities with a commitment to antiracism work.
- Incorporate antiracist training through teacher-to-teacher mentoring.
- Develop a definition of the characteristics and behaviors of an antiracist student.

https://bit.ly/3vCT5ld

Their past work includes book discussion groups based on the following texts and action steps connected with the book studies:

- *White Fragility* by Robin DiAngelo
- *Case Studies on Diversity and Social Justice Education* by Paul C. Gorski and Seema G. Pothini
- *Being the Change: Lessons and Strategies to Teach Social Comprehension* by Sara K. Ahmed
- *We Got This: Equity, Access, and the Quest to Be Who Our Students Need Us to Be* by Cornelius Minor

# Breathe and Reflect

How might you partner with colleagues in your school/district to create an ABAR professional learning community as Lina, Karen, and Kerry have? Use this space to reflect on the names of colleagues who might be interested in such a professional learning community. ▪

_____

_____

_____

_____

_____

_____

_____

_____

_____

_____

_____

_____

_____

_____

_____

_____

_____

_____

_____

_____

_____

_____

_____

_____

_____

# Overcoming Internal Resistance: Taking Responsibility for Our Biases and What Feeds Them

It's essential that we spend some time thinking about how to respond to the resistance that we'll encounter in ourselves. We all have cognitive biases. Our minds tend to notice patterns, create categories and shortcuts based on patterns, and form opinions and beliefs as a result of what we notice. Here are some of the types of unconscious biases that can be harmful personally—and particularly in our work with students:

- *Anchoring bias* causes us to rely too heavily on the first piece of information we are given about a topic.

- *Blind-spot bias* causes us to recognize the impact of biases on the judgment of others while failing to see the impact of biases on one's own judgment.

- *Confirmation bias* is the tendency to search for, interpret, favor, and recall information in a way that confirms or supports one's prior beliefs or values.

- *Conservatism bias* refers to the tendency to revise one's belief insufficiently when presented with new evidence.

- *Recency bias* favors recent events over historic ones.

- *Selective-perception bias* is the tendency not to notice and more quickly forget stimuli that cause emotional discomfort and contradict our prior beliefs.

Unaddressed and unchecked unconscious biases can lead to harm in relationships that can show up as racial microaggressions. Racial microaggressions are frequent (not small) slights and harm done to people from historically and currently marginalized groups. Microaggressions can show up in several ways:

- Microinvalidations, characterized by communications that exclude, negate, or nullify the psychological thoughts, feelings, or experiential reality of a Person of Color

- Microinsults, characterized by communications that convey rudeness and insensitivity and demean a person's racial heritage or identity

- Microassaults, explicit racial derogations characterized primarily by a verbal or nonverbal attack meant to hurt the intended victim through name-calling, avoidant behavior, or purposeful discriminatory actions

Figure 4.3 shows examples of how microaggressions may appear in majority-White classrooms and school communities.

## FIGURE 4.3 Three Types of Microaggressions

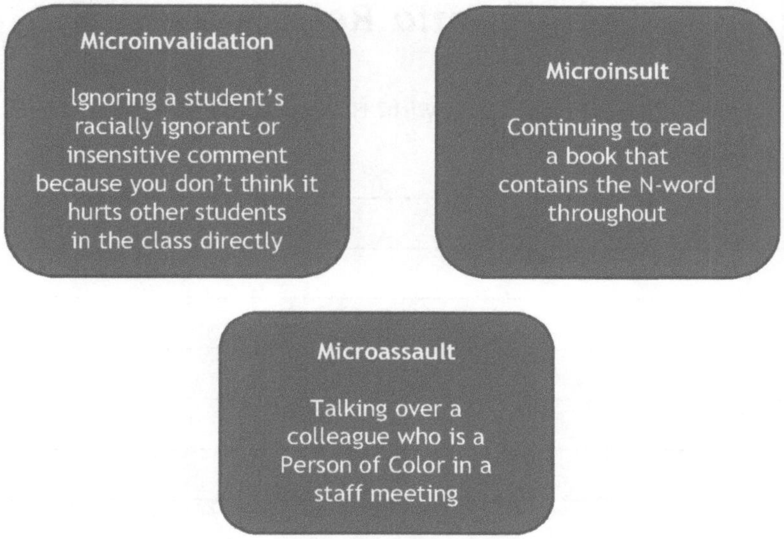

**Microinvalidation**

Ignoring a student's racially ignorant or insensitive comment because you don't think it hurts other students in the class directly

**Microinsult**

Continuing to read a book that contains the N-word throughout

**Microassault**

Talking over a colleague who is a Person of Color in a staff meeting

We can decrease racial microaggressions by interrogating and addressing our implicit biases as well as exposing the sources of inaccurate perceptions and beliefs about people with whom we don't share the same racial identity.

# Breathe and Reflect

What are some of the biases you struggle with? How have you seen those biases lead to microaggressions? ▪

_____

_____

_____

_____

_____

_____

_____

_____

_____

_____

_____

_____

_____

_____

_____

_____

_____

_____

_____

_____

_____

_____

_____

_____

_____

_____

_____

_____

_____

Senninger's Learning Model (ThemPra Social Pedagogy n.d.) offers a helpful frame when it comes to laying the foundation of effective learning opportunities, especially around matters related to race. We need to be able to move from our *comfort zone*, where we feel secure and take few risks, to the *learning zone* where we expand what's familiar by discovering new things. Beyond the learning zone is the *panic zone*, which we need to avoid. In this zone, learning and curiosity are blocked by fear because we expend most of our energy managing negative emotions. (See Figure 4.4.)

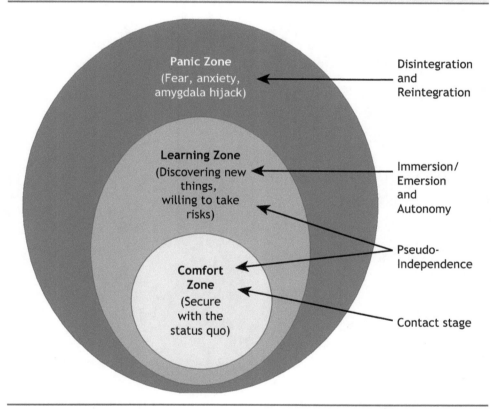

FIGURE 4.4 Senninger's Learning Model

Awareness of comfort, learning, and panic zones is a critical consideration, as failing to lay an effective foundation for critical conversations can push people into a panic zone where our ABAR work can face more resistance than necessary. Although human anatomy and physiology was one of my favorite undergraduate college classes, the first encounter with the word *amygdala* I can remember and understanding of the term *amygdala hijack* was reading Zaretta Hammond's *Culturally Responsive Teaching and the Brain* and hearing her speak for the first time at the Initiatives for Developing Equity and Achievement for Students

(IDEAS) conference in 2019. Amygdala hijack, according to Timothy J. Legg, CRNP (Holland 2021), is a sudden illogical and irrational overreaction triggered by a stressful situation. Basically this occurs when the amygdala—which activates our primal flight-or-flight response—overpowers the frontal lobe where thinking, reason, and decision-making occur.

I am not a psychologist, but I think it's fair to say that we are witnessing quite a bit of amygdala hijacking at school board/committee meetings, in race-related professional development spaces across the United States, in voting booths as legislation is considered and passed that would keep students from truly grappling with the history of the United States, and with regard to engaging with students about race in the United States.

# Breathe and Reflect

When have you been resistant to change? What was at the heart of this resistance? Use this space to reflect on a time when you experienced an amygdala hijack. How did you navigate through it? ■

_____

_____

_____

_____

_____

_____

_____

_____

_____

_____

_____

_____

_____

_____

_____

_____

_____

_____

_____

_____

_____

_____

_____

_____

_____

# PREPARING FOR EXTERNAL RESISTANCE

We're living in a time where there are some who are responding to the growing emphasis on ABAR, diverse, equitable, and inclusive approaches to instruction by railing against critical race theory, labeling it as Marxist indoctrination. As I am writing, Republican lawmakers in nearly half of the states in the United States have proposed or passed legislation to limit the teaching of concepts such as racial equity and White privilege. Those who are protesting say that they are doing so because they believe that critical race theory is being taught in schools and that White students are being made to feel guilty for being White. They have also expressed concern that resources like *The 1619 Project* include false information about the history of the United States. Unfortunately, many are engaging in this resistance, fueled and equipped by groups that have never read or researched what they believe they are resisting.

Something similar happened around the time that NFL player Colin Kaepernick began his protest at football games. Kaepernick was very clear for the duration of his protest that he was standing and then kneeling to protest police violence against Black bodies. The narrative shifted away from his stated intentions to become something altogether different—that he was unpatriotic, hated the United States and the military, and that he intended to disrespect the U.S. flag and national anthem.

As Carol Anderson highlighted in *White Rage*, racial progress has historically been met with severe backlash. We know this, and because we do, we can anticipate the resistance and prepare for it by educating and preparing ourselves. Some of this polarization can find its way into your classroom, and you will need to be prepared to respond to it.

Howard Stevenson (2017), in his "How to Resolve Racially Stressful Situations" 2017 TED Talk, offers the CLCBE approach—*calculate, locate, communicate, breathe, and exhale*—that can help us to respond to the race-based stress we experience when we're in the panic zone:

*Calculate*: Identify what you're feeling and how intense it is on a scale of 1 to 10.

*Locate:* Identify where in your body you're experiencing the feeling specifically, like "I feel my anger manifesting in my unsettled stomach" or "I notice that I'm holding my breath when I feel anxiety." Pinpointing where the feeling is precisely can make it easier to reduce that stress.

*Communicate:* Articulate the story you're telling yourself in the moment and what your mind sees.

Then *breathe* in and *exhale* slowly. (Rosati 2020)

I am reminded that those who engaged in nonviolent resistance during the Civil Rights Movement did not do so without preparing for their encounters (as Howard Stevenson recommends as well) with those who opposed them. This is important to note, because just as it can be a natural human response to avoid conflict, it is a natural human response to retaliate or respond in kind when someone is attempting to harm you. During the Civil Rights Movement of the 1960s, there was training "school" where nonviolent protesters would prepare to remain nonviolent by engaging in social dramas where they'd experience humiliation and abuse like having smoke blown in their faces, being hit with newspapers, having their hair pulled, having chairs jostled, being verbally assaulted with racial epithets, and having coffee poured on them.

https://bit.ly/3vCzf9H

It remains true that taking the time to prepare is essential. It's important to be as proactive as possible instead of reactive. When we wait to respond to racially charged content and incidents until they happen, reaching resolution can be more challenging than it needs to be. The Learning for Justice *Speak Up at School* resource outlines four potential responses to practice in prepa-

https://bit.ly/3L85apb

ration for when you and/or students encounter biased, microaggressive, prejudiced, and/or stereotypical comments or ideas:

- **Interrupt:** Especially if harm is being done by someone's words or actions, those words or actions need to be interrupted immediately with a comment like "What you just said is hurtful, and this is not the way we treat students in our school." These comments should not disempower the person who is being harmed, so it's important to make sure when interrupting it is not an attempt to save anyone but to stand alongside and stand up for a commitment to treating everyone with respect, honor, and dignity.

- **Question:** Ask the person making the comment or expressing the idea to explain their reasoning. Comments like "That hasn't been my experience. Can you say more about what you mean when you say that?" This approach should be carefully considered to make sure that additional harm is not likely to occur.

- **Educate:** Let the person know that what they have expressed is inaccurate. For example, if someone says "I don't see color," a response that could educate might be, "When you say that you don't see color, your intention may be to convey that you don't see anything wrong with someone's color, but it could make someone feel like you're trying to avoid a part of their identity that is very important to pay attention to." With this approach, you should be sure that your motivation is to partner with the person to help their intent to match their impact and not to patronize or belittle.

- **Echo:** If someone else has already spoken up in the face of a hurtful comment, you can state your agreement with them in an act of solidarity.

These strategies can be helpful in classroom conversations as well as in situations outside the classroom, such as parent conferences and staff meetings.

## Breathe and Reflect

Which of the *Speak Up at School* recommended responses do you think will best support you and your students as you prepare to respond to biased, microaggressive, prejudiced, stereotypical comments, and/or negative peer or group pressure and make decisions about how and when to take a stand against injustice? What is at risk if you don't engage in this preparation? ■

_____

_____

_____

_____

_____

_____

_____

_____

_____

_____

_____

_____

_____

_____

_____

_____

_____

_____

_____

_____

_____

_____

_____

_____

_____

# Creating a Brave Space for Critical Classroom Conversations

At a 2018 Equity Literacy Approach: Becoming a Threat to Inequity in Classrooms and Schools workshop, Paul Gorski said that in order to dismantle inequitable systems, we need three things: goodwill, skill, and will to make changes (*the equity literacy approach*). Goodwill is clear. Most educators are teachers for beautiful reasons. We believe that all children should have access to rich, engaging learning opportunities where they can lay the foundation of becoming informed citizens who are equipped to have a positive impact on the world. Some of us are teachers because we come from a long line of teachers, and it's a profession that we've come to love. Some of us became teachers to be the teachers we wish we had during our own K–12 experiences. Whatever our reasons, we have the goodwill to play such an integral role in the lives of children. We need to keep working, though, on building *skill* to ensure that we can create and sustain such learning experiences, and we need the *will* to endure in the face of difficulty. Throughout the workshop, Gorski encouraged participants to "fix injustice, not kids." We must, for the sake of the children, be doggedly determined to keep pushing beyond the distractions toward healing, awareness, and solidarity as we work together toward a better world.

Learning to have critical conversations with students involves change, and change is hard, because, as my colleague Darnisa Amante-Jackson of the Disruptive Equity Education Project shared in one of her workshops, change involves loss. It may be important to consider the stages of grief too: denial, anger, bargaining, depression, and acceptance. We have to give up a familiar way of thinking and being so that the ground of our hearts and minds is fertile and ready for something new to grow. It *is* good, but it doesn't necessarily *feel* good.

Change also involves conflict as we grapple with learning and implementing a new way of engaging in instruction with our students. It's not natural to give up ways of thinking about being that we've grown accustomed to. If you're anything like me, conflict makes you very uncomfortable. When it comes to a fight, flight, freeze, or fawn/appease response, my default setting is to flee and get as far away from difficult feelings as possible. And with my tendency toward flight can often come silence. Clint Smith (2014) shares the following in his 2014 TED Talk, "The Danger of Silence":

> We spend so much time listening to the things people are saying that
> we rarely pay attention to the things they don't. Silence is the residue of
> fear. It is feeling your flaws gut-wrench guillotine your tongue. It is the
> air retreating from your chest because it doesn't feel safe in your lungs.

Smith (2014) explains the ways he challenges students—and himself—to "work together to fill those spaces, to recognize them, to name them, to understand that they don't have to be sources of shame." In order to help White students to experience the benefit of more windows, we must intentionally shift our instructional practices. This begins with creating a brave space in which to do this work with our students.

Having critical conversations about race with students of all ages begins with building trust. The activities, resources, and tools explored in Chapter 2 help to lay the foundation of trust building. When a teacher has shared their personal stories, histories, interests and created a space where students can do the same, teachers have the relational capital needed to engage in more challenging conversations.

I use the term *brave space* instead of *safe space* here intentionally, because, as mentioned earlier in the chapter, change is not always comfortable, and so many of us equate safety with comfort. A brave space, however, pushes us to lean into instead of shy away from discomfort, knowing that growth is on the other side.

## CO-CREATING CLASSROOM AGREEMENTS

Part of creating a brave space with students includes co-creating agreements for your learning community. I stay away from the word *norms* because it implies that there are some predetermined expectations for how we engage as a learning community that are "normal," and that should not be true.

Parker Palmer's "Circle of Trust Touchstones" have been very helpful in my racial consciousness journey and as I facilitate learning spaces for participants. Some of the touchstones include:

https://bit.ly/3OsHIoD

- Speak your truth in ways that respect other people's truth.

- Learn to respond to others with honest, open questions.

- When the going gets rough, turn to wonder.

- Trust and learn from the silence.

- Know that it's possible.

In *Mindful of Race: Transforming Racism from the Inside Out* (King 2018), Ruth King states that racism is a heart disease that is curable, and she shows readers how to engage in the healing process by connecting mindfulness practices with racial healing (hence the Breathe and Reflect sections of this book). Frameworks like the touchstones can help us to maintain this focus as adult learners. We want to learn and model the same practices with our students and, in doing so, increase our emotional intelligence and make it possible for them to do the same.

Co-creating brave spaces community agreements with students offers a way of building and sustaining a trusting learning community where you can regularly discuss hard things. It involves asking students to identify times when they've felt comfortable sharing their ideas and questions in class, and what made them feel comfortable, and also times when they've withheld ideas and questions and what was happening at those times.

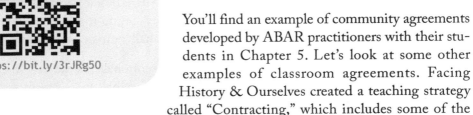
https://bit.ly/3rJRg50

You'll find an example of community agreements developed by ABAR practitioners with their students in Chapter 5. Let's look at some other examples of classroom agreements. Facing History & Ourselves created a teaching strategy called "Contracting," which includes some of the following recommendations for classroom agreements (you can link to this resource using the QR code in the margin):

- Listen with respect. Try to understand what someone is saying before rushing to judgment. If you don't understand something, ask a question.

- If you do not feel safe making a comment or asking a question, write the thought in your journal. You can share the idea with your teacher first and together come up with a safe way to share the idea.

- If someone says an idea or question that helps your own learning, say thank you.

- If someone says something that hurts or offends you, do not attack the person. Acknowledge that the comment—not the person—hurt your feelings and explain why.

- Put-downs are never okay.

- Share the talking time—provide room for others to speak.

- Do not interrupt others while they are speaking.

The Learning for Justice's *Let's Talk* guide, referenced earlier in the chapter, offers an example of community agreements, which includes the following:

- *I will listen to understand, not just to respond.*

- *I will use evidence, including facts or my own experience, to support my point of view.*

- *I will not make assumptions about the experiences of others.*

- *I will challenge and question ideas or assumptions, not people.*

- *I will ask for clarification when I'm unclear about what's been said.* (24)

Other helpful agreements can be recognizing the difference between intent and impact and between evidence and experience. It's also important to ensure that students know that it is not only okay but expected that we will make mistakes, and to feel confident that their missteps won't lead to them being disconnected from the learning community. A friend and colleague, during a collaborative meeting, talked about the importance of having *at bats*. We don't always hit a home run while batting. Sometimes we hit a foul ball, and sometimes we swing and miss. The attempts are as critical and foundational as the times we make contact with the ball that leads to getting on base. Sometimes it'll be first. Sometimes second, third, or all the way home. All at bats are an essential part of the growth process (D. Guerrero, personal communication).

## AGREEING ABOUT HOW TO DISAGREE

It's also important for you to determine how you'll address disagreements. In addition to your co-created agreements, this exploration will give you and students touchstones to come back to.

As you co-create a set of classroom agreements, you can build on your students' social-emotional skills by having them explore what they want your classroom conversations to *look*, *sound*, and *feel*, especially when there are disagreements. Explore this more deeply with students using the following scenarios, also included in the Facing History & Ourselves "Contracting" resource:

- When we have an idea but do not feel comfortable sharing it out loud, we can . . .

- When someone says something that might be confusing or offensive, we can . . .

- If we read or watch something that makes us feel sad or angry, we can . . .

These tools are needed to ensure that students are socially and emotionally prepared by teaching social-emotional skills; modeling positive relationships and conflict resolution skills; focusing on understanding and appreciating differences, challenging bias, and inclusion; and encouraging students to be upstanders.

## PREPARING FOR CRITICAL CONVERSATIONS

Preparing for critical conversations about race involves teachers becoming aware of the topics that evoke the most comfort and discomfort, the topics that most impact them and their students as well as reflecting on which topics they know the most and least about and which topics you have the most and least experience with. It also involves engaging in self-assessment to identify your vulnerabilities, strengths, and needs, and this resource provides those tools. You can ask yourself the following questions:

- What topics are you uncomfortable discussing? What is the source of your discomfort?

- Name a time you felt strong and capable, and identify what you can apply from that experience to times where you feel more vulnerable and not as capable.

- What support do you need after you've made a mistake with students?

We want to create and sustain brave spaces in our classrooms. There will be some times when, despite your best efforts, these conversations may not go the way you plan. We are all people, and we all have bad days, stresses, distractions, and things happening in our lives outside of school that impact how we are in school. As much as it depends on you, as often as possible, try not to hinder an effectively brave space by neglecting to engage in careful preparation. And when you mess up (and you will—we all do), forgive yourself and keep going.

# Breathe and Reflect

What are some agreements you would like to consider as you prepare to create a brave space in your classroom? Knowing that you will make mistakes in this work, what will you do to process your mistakes and forgive yourself so that you can sustain your ABAR instructional practices? Name some people in your life who can provide you with encouragement and support. ▪

_____

_____

_____

_____

_____

_____

_____

_____

_____

_____

_____

_____

_____

_____

_____

_____

_____

_____

_____

_____

_____

_____

_____

_____

# PART 2

# HOW TO PROVIDE WHITE STUDENTS WITH MORE WINDOWS

# CHAPTER 5

# Opening Windows Into Overlooked Contributions, Histories, and Experiences

## Content That Expands Understanding

As part of a course titled Anti-Racist School Practices to Support the Success of All Students facilitated by Initiatives for Developing Equity and Achievement for Students (IDEAS) instructors JoAnne Kazis and Johnny Cole, participants were led through an exercise where they were given time to list as many People of Color in the following categories:

- Mathematicians and scientists

- Athletes

- Politicians

- Actors and musicians

I felt frustrated, because most of the mathematicians, scientists, and politicians that came to mind for me were White men. When Johnny and JoAnne shared the word cloud generated from our responses, George Washington Carver, Neil deGrasse Tyson, Katherine Johnson, Barack Obama, Ayanna Pressley, and

Alexandria Ocasio-Cortez showed up on some lists, but the list of athletes, actors, and musicians were far more robust than the lists of mathematicians, scientists, and politicians. And even the lists that were generated were shorter than they seemed, considering that any misspellings of names and acronyms appeared as separate entries (e.g., AOC and Alexandria Ocasio-Cortez). Figure 5.1 shows the word clouds generated in this exercise.

**FIGURE 5.1  Word Clouds Listing Notable People of Color in Various Categories**

## Athletes of Color

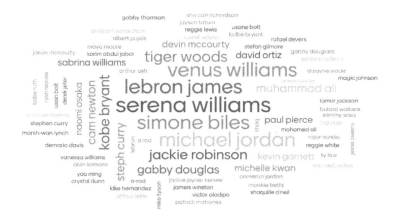

## Mathematicians & Scientists of Color

# Musicians/Actors of Color

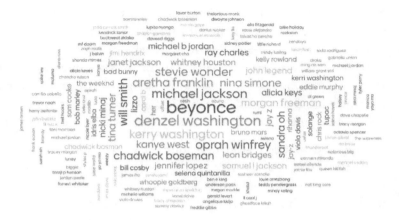

# Politicians of Color

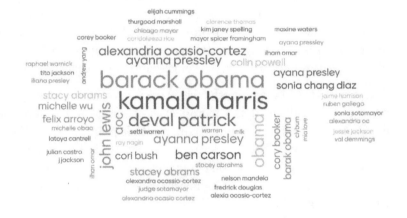

When it came to listing athletes and musicians, it was a lot easier to list Black and Brown people, depending on what sports and music genres came to mind; for example, there were fewer listed with classical music and golf, but thanks to athletes like Serena Williams and Naomi Osaka, the tennis references were a little more racially diverse. The same was true with actors, depending on what movies and TV shows we tend to watch.

I had a similar experience in another workshop when participants were asked to name the first country we could think of starting with the letter *D*. Without fail, most of us chose Denmark. Perhaps one or two people said the Democratic Republic of the

Congo or the Dominican Republic; the facilitators shared that in another workshop, not even the participants from the Dominican Republic named their own country—they, too, chose Denmark. I don't think anyone named Djibouti or Dominica.

So what does this indicate? The results of both of these exercises show how White people have long been centered in all spaces—music, sports, mathematics, science, politics, and the like—and that all of us, whether White or a Person of Color, have difficulty calling to mind an equal number of standouts from marginalized populations. This is not by accident but by design. Antiracist work requires us first to acknowledge the ways Whiteness is centered—an attempt to exclude all other people and contributions from history, current discourse, and ultimately, power.

It's important for educators to feature the contributions of people from marginalized groups who are not typically featured in traditional White-centric curriculum and those who contribute to fields where they are not usually celebrated by profiling Black and Brown mathematicians, scientists, engineers, and politicians without tokenizing or focusing on typical fields like acting, music, and sports. Further, we must be sure to explore the point of view and agency of all involved stakeholders to avoid the negative impact of telling a single story when teaching history (e.g., *How did enslaved people resist enslavement? How did the Indigenous respond to the Indian Removal Act?*). We need to incorporate literature featuring people from marginalized groups doing everyday things in multiple genres (e.g., Black and Brown characters in fantasy and science fiction stories, playing in the snow, having fun with a pet, learning how to play an instrument, and trying to run from the moon) instead of only focusing on struggle, challenges, and injustices.

A critical part of being an effective ABAR practitioner means ensuring that students can critically analyze the impact of historical and current events and engage in perspective-taking and understand multiple points of view. These learning experiences will give White students the tools needed to move from unconscious incompetence, where they don't know what they don't know and have to commit a good deal of cognitive effort to decentering themselves to conscious competence, where centering the stories of all people is as second nature as riding a bike without having to think about balancing, pedaling, steering, or braking.

Prior to the beginning of K–12 learning experiences, children are inundated with the message that Whiteness is the dominant culture. This extends from the images in the media and children's books to the content we engage students with in schools. This chapter will support you as you provide students with regular opportunities to engage with accurate and inclusive history and content that represents the lives, interests, contributions, and experiences of other races of people. You will also be equipped to support students to ask questions instead of making assumptions about social issues, to engage in productive struggle as they challenge false narratives about people from marginalized groups, and to adopt a growth mindset about their ability to continue this learning. This work will help students to see themselves as belonging to the larger human family.

# Breathe and Reflect

What is your experience with celebrating Black, Indigenous, and People of Color (BIPOC) during specific heritage months (e.g., Black History Month, Arab American History Month, Asian American and Pacific Islander Heritage Month, Hispanic Heritage Month, Indigenous Peoples Month)? How would you like to expand your students' experiences celebrating the histories and contributions of People of Color throughout the year? ■

_____

_____

_____

_____

_____

_____

_____

_____

_____

_____

_____

_____

_____

_____

_____

_____

_____

_____

_____

_____

_____

_____

_____

## CONNECTING ACROSS DIFFERENCE

By incorporating antibias, antiracist (ABAR) practices and centering more learning experiences around traditionally underrepresented groups, teachers will learn to effectively engage students in learning about the contributions, histories, and lives of people who are racially different throughout the school year—and not just during designated history/heritage months.

In the summer of 2018, I had the privilege of participating in the Multicultural Teaching Institute at the Meadowbrook School in Weston, Massachusetts. I don't know about you, but when I go to a conference and there is high-quality swag as soon as you walk in, I get excited. The binder they had prepared for participants was on point, as was the tumbler we were all gifted with. One of the other gifts was the invitation to include our pronouns on our name tags. I didn't realize how much of a gift it was that day, because as a cisgender heterosexual woman, I hadn't been very mindful of my pronouns up until that point. I didn't have to be. I see my gender and sexual orientation mirrored back to me all the time. Additionally, during the institute, I didn't meet anyone whose pronouns differed from the pronouns I would have used without knowing, so my mindset stayed pretty much the same. I did wonder how someone who also identified as Christian would respond to seeing me share my pronouns. In my experience up until that point, most people I knew who professed Christian faith did not discuss gender identity, and most of what I heard in those spaces espoused heteronormativity and cisgenderism.

I didn't encounter the cognitive dissonance that accompanies a shift toward an expanded understanding of gender identity until I was part of the White Privilege Symposium in the fall of 2018 where I first met someone who shared with me that their pronouns were they and them. I will call them Lily. I committed a significant amount of cognitive effort to trying to ensure that I did not misgender my new friend. However, when I started to listen to them share about their experiences and frustration as someone who is gender nonconforming instead of trying to be perfect with my pronoun usage, I began to learn. For example, when they shared their disappointment about the gender-neutral bathrooms being farther away from the main meeting room than the gendered bathrooms, I initially wondered why Lily didn't go to the women's bathroom, since, in my mind, they presented as female. But then I asked myself how I'd feel if the nearest bathrooms were labeled *For White Women Only*? This is something my ancestors faced not too long ago. I could go into that bathroom, but I would feel excluded and potentially concerned for my safety.

When we went to the same breakout session shortly after we met, our facilitator entered the room and greeted participants by saying "Hello, ladies and gentlemen!" In the past, I wouldn't have noticed how that greeting interrupts belonging for people who don't conform to the gender binary. I noticed it then. Now my pronouns appear regularly. They are in my e-mail signatures and on my social media profiles. I need to remain diligent to ensure that sharing my pronouns isn't performative. It's the same with Indigenous land acknowledgments. It's not a box to check but a way of seeing the world.

One of the best examples I've seen of teaching students to authentically connect with one another across differences is the partnership between Melissa Collins and Michael J. Dunlea, both elementary educators who are both friends and colleagues. Melissa is a National Board Certified teacher who works with second-grade students at the John P. Freeman Optional School in Memphis, Tennessee. Michael is also a National Board Certified teacher who teaches third grade at the Tabernacle Elementary School in the Tabernacle Township School District, which is a rural preK–8 public school district in Tabernacle, New Jersey. Melissa and all of her students identify as Black, and Michael and all of his students identify as White. Michael's students met Melissa's students through Empatico.

> Although Empatico is highlighted in this section, there are other platforms and tools that can help facilitate cross-classroom communication and relationship building. Platforms such as Edmodo.com and ePals.com are geared directly for schools, and Google Hangouts or Skype might offer similar functionality. Talk with your school's technology director to learn what's possible, and please always prioritize student safety and privacy.

Empatico (Empatico.com) is a free online tool that connects classrooms around the world, empowering teachers and students to explore the world through experiences that spark curiosity, kindness, and empathy. The online tool combines video with activities designed to foster meaningful connections among students ages six to eleven, and Empatico provided the students with the opportunity to mitigate the impact of segregation by building authentic relationships with one another. Melissa and Michael's classes connected with one another online and engaged in learning assignments that they shared with one another. They even surprised Michael's students by arranging for them to meet Melissa in person. Melissa traveled 1,000 miles to meet them.

https://bit.ly/38ejNbY

When I interviewed Michael, he shared how illuminating it was to notice the difference between how his students processed Martin Luther King Jr.'s birthday and how Melissa's students processed it. Melissa's class, populated by Black students, experience Black history as a vital part of their lives and stories and feel the pressure of violence against Black bodies imminently; Michael's students, all of whom are White, though they have had some exposure to King's words, have not lived with the anxiety of violence yet want to appreciate and love all people. In other words, the White students were looking through the window but had not fully understood the lived experiences of their Black peers. In Michael's words:

> We had them all making posters for Martin Luther King. We've done this for three or four years where around his birthday, they create their own signs with their own messages. We call it the *I Have a Dream* lesson where they all say what their dream would be. We frame it with the history of Martin Luther King's dream. Prior to George Floyd, we had a nice balance of kids asking for racial harmony and safer, cleaner worlds with no pollution. Post–George Floyd, almost every child in Melissa's class was saying, "Black Lives Matter! Don't kill us!" And the White kids were still saying, "Let's all love each other!" It's like they have on rose colored glasses because they're not dealing with the reality that the other communities are. I had a student who created a sign that said, "All lives matter." She didn't mean it the way some people have intended it as a counter to Black Lives Matter. She meant it from the pure heart of a seven-year-old. She genuinely believes, especially after making friends in Melissa's class, that all lives matter, but if someone sees her poster out of context, it could come across like she's sharing a harmful sentiment that she heard at home. But we want her to continue to truly believe that all lives matter.

One of the benefits of students connecting with students who are racially different is that they have the opportunity to move beyond false narratives and stereotypical ideas to building authentic relationships, being able to consider new perspectives, and to discovering what we have in common as well. For a White student to learn about experiences of People of Color from People of Color is a powerful way to help undo the harm caused by our segregated communities.

Michael shared, "As a classroom teacher we are often dedicated to providing for our students what they need most. Sometimes in our highly segregated communities what they need most is just a chance to spend time with people who are different." Michael explained that Empatico provided a chance to merge two very different classrooms into one group. Michael and Melissa paired students who became much more than pen pals; they became friends by sharing reading time, and they met several times just to chat over the platform. Michael explained, "Young minds are plastic, their biases are still in the forming stages or are not even present yet. These friendships provide me with hope that they will act as a personal rejection to the seeds of racism or hate that will be planted later." Giving students real experiences where they meet and become friends with students who identify with different racial backgrounds can keep negative biases from taking root down the road. It makes the world a smaller place where we can spend time with people who look and sound different but have more in common than is initially appreciated," explained Michael.

Reflecting on her experience, Melissa shared, "Living in the South as a young Black girl, I had very little interaction with White students. I had minimum connections with another race or culture until college. I had to learn how to foster a relationship with someone who was different from me if I was going to survive. When I returned to Memphis to teach, I entered a predominantly Black and Brown classroom. I was not surprised, but not much about my community had changed."

Melissa explained that helping her students to connect with kids from a different racial background was a dream she held as an educator, and collaborating online through Empatico.com helped the dream become reality. "I thought, what if Michael and I could inspire others to step out of their comfort zone to promote racial harmony for today's students? If we continue to do this each year, we will create current leaders who would fight for justice."

Melissa continued, "The connection with Michael's class changed the racial narrative for my students and others to spark empathy, curiosity, and critical thinking skills. . . . The students learned that they had commonalities such as favorite colors, family dynamics, and activities. However, they had some differences: food, festivals, holidays, dialect, or communities. The unique aspect of the connection is that they learned to appreciate each other regardless of their differences. Often, our geographic locations, culture, and traditions shape us, but we must realize as a nation, positive connections help to create our democracy."

In Michael's experience, "Teachers, especially White teachers, need to push past the fear of making a mistake. We want to change the world but are afraid to get started on deconstructing the systems of racism. Developing and nurturing relationships is the first step in getting to a space where the knowledge can overcome the fear. Our students, Black and White, desperately need us to get into our discomfort and get moving on this."

It's important to keep in mind that you may not need technology to make such connections happen, but there are many tools at our fingertips that can make it easier to connect with a classroom whose student population comes from a different racial background than your own. I recommend doing some research through social media groups that you trust, asking simply who might be interested in forming a cross-classroom connection such as this, then determining (with consultation with your school's technology team) if Empatico or another platform can help you get started.

# Breathe and Reflect

If you are working in a school with mostly White students who are between the ages of six and eleven, use this space to reflect on the possibility of implementing Empatico with your students. If your students are older, how might you provide them opportunities to connect with people who are racially different? ■

_____

_____

_____

_____

_____

_____

_____

_____

_____

_____

_____

_____

_____

_____

_____

_____

_____

_____

_____

_____

_____

_____

_____

_____

_____

_____

# LEARNING OR REDISCOVERING US HISTORY

As mentioned in earlier chapters, many of us, unless we had atypical or extraordinary school experiences, did not learn accurate US history. Thankfully, we have the primary source documents, research, texts, podcasts, articles, documentaries, and museums that provide us with the information we didn't receive in our K–12 experiences. We can't always take students to a museum, but there are a number of resources to use that can help students to think critically about the US history they've learned; see the online companion for a list of these resources: resources.corwin.com/openwindows.

We also have the spoken word of brilliant scholars and poets like Clint Smith—author of *Counting Descent* (2016) and *How the Word Is Passed: A Reckoning of the History of Slavery Across America* (2021)—that teachers can use as an introductory instructional resource. Here is the transcript of Smith's 2016 spoken word titled *History Reconsidered*, with suggestions for instruction following. (Because this spoken-word piece makes reference to sexual assault, be sure to take appropriate measures to share the piece with families ahead of time and prepare students with a trigger warning.)

## *History Reconsidered* by Clint Smith (2016)

Letter to five of the presidents who owned slaves while they were in office:

George Washington, when you won the revolution, how many of your soldiers did you send from the battlefield to the cottonfield? How many had to trade in their rifles for plows? Can you blame the slaves who ran away to fight for the British because at least the Red Coats were honest about their oppression.

Thomas Jefferson, when you told Sally Hemings that you would free her children if she remained your mistress, did you think there was honor in your ultimatum? Did you think we wouldn't be able to recognize the assault in your signature? Does raping your slave when you disguise it as bribery make it less of a crime? When you wrote the Declaration of Independence, did you ever intend for Black people to have freedom over their bodies?

James Madison, when you wrote to Congress that Black people should count as $\frac{3}{5}$ of a person, how long did you have to look at your slaves to figure out the math? Was it easy to chop them up? Did you think they'd be happy being more than just half-human?

*(Continued)*

(Continued)

James Monroe, when you proposed sending slaves back to Africa, did Black bodies feel like rented tools? When you branded them, did the scar on their chest include an expiration date? When you named the country Liberia, were you trying to be ironic? Does this really count as liberation?

Andrew Jackson, was the Trail of Tears not enough for you? Was killing Cherokee, Choctaw, Creek, Seminoles not enough to quench your imperialism?

How many Brown bodies do you have to bulldoze before you can call it progress Mr. Washington, Jefferson, Madison, Monroe, Jackson, when you put your hand on the Bible and swore to protect this country, let's be honest in who you were talking about. When the first Independence Day fireworks set the sky aflame, don't forget where we were watching from.

So when you remember Jefferson's genius, don't forget the slaves who built the bookshelves in his library. When you remember Jackson's victories in war, don't forget what he was fighting to preserve. When you sing that this country was founded on freedom, don't forget the duet of shackles dragging against the ground.

My entire life I've been taught how perfect this country was. But no one ever told me about the pages torn out of my textbooks. How Black and Brown bodies have been bludgeoned for three centuries, and find no place in the curriculum. Oppression doesn't disappear just because you decided not to teach us that chapter. If you only hear one side of the story, at some point, you have to question who the writer is.

---

Clint Smith, "History Reconsidered." *Youtube*. Permission granted by The Gernert Company https:// www.youtube.com/watch?v=rEVowYqRAJE

https://bit.ly/37wz4Vz

You can implement this poem as an instructional resource with your students by initially having them listen to Clint Smith reciting it, followed by these instructional moves:

- Repeated reading is a helpful tool when it comes to helping students build their comprehension skills. Provide students with a copy of the poem, and have them read along while you (or someone else) reads the poem aloud.

- Have students engage in an independent close reading of the poem, and annotate the text, indicating unfamiliar words, connections, surprising details, questions, and recording their thinking and questions in the margins. You can choose symbols for the annotations (e.g., a circle for an unknown word, a question mark for questions), and if you have enough colored pencils, you can have students color-code the different annotations.

- Put students into small groups to discuss what they recorded after their close reading.

- As a way to wrap up the lesson, you can have students share some of the things they noticed, and use their questions, the unfamiliar words, and connections as a type of formative assessment to help you shape subsequent lessons.

This poem brings up historical names and events that students may have never heard of before, so it would be helpful to allow time for researching and processing unknown content. You can have small groups of students jigsaw articles about the content in small groups with each group (see Chapter 6 for a closer look at the jigsaw strategy). Here's what it might look like; all of these articles are linked from this book's online companion (resources.corwin.com/openwindows):

- Group A can read "How Enslaved Men Who Fought for the British Were Promised Freedom" on History.com.

- Group B can read a selected passage from Monticello.org's "The Life of Sally Hemings."

- Group C can read *Teen Vogue*'s "How the Electoral College Is Tied to Slavery and the Three-Fifths Compromise."

- Group D can read and watch PBS Learning Media's *A Short History of Liberia.*

- Group E can read PBS Learning Media's *Trail of Tears | We Shall Remain*

As an extension, you can implement the National Park Service lesson plan about the Trail of Tears. The lesson plan includes an essential question, objectives, background information, vocabulary, and instructional materials. This resource is also linked in the online companion to this book: resources.corwin.com/ openwindows.

https://bit.ly/38eTt13

Once they've had the opportunity to explore the content more deeply, share what they notice and wonder in a whole-group discussion. This approach will allow students to unpack this content in a way that's thoughtful of classroom agreements and touchstones you will have established.

# Breathe and Reflect

After reading *History Reconsidered*, what are some things you notice and wonder based on the history you learned about the United States in your K-12 experience? ■

_____

_____

_____

_____

_____

_____

_____

_____

_____

_____

_____

_____

_____

_____

_____

_____

_____

_____

_____

_____

_____

_____

_____

_____

# Building Radical Empathy

My husband and I lived in Boston for the first eight years of our marriage. Four years into our marriage, we had our daughter, Serena. A year later, our son, Cairo, was born. As the children grew, we needed to branch out beyond our two-bedroom apartment, so we bought a home in a community not too far outside of Boston. This community appealed to us because we both wanted to raise our children in a multicultural community. When our daughter was five, and our son was four, a church in a neighboring town was hosting a fair. You know the fairs with the bouncy houses and face painting? My husband was busy that day, but I looked forward to taking the kids to the fair. The neighboring town was not as racially diverse as our town. Perhaps that should have been a red flag for me, but it wasn't. I was a mom looking forward to having fun with her children.

Like the other children their age, Serena and Cairo were anxious to get into the bouncy house. They took off their shoes, lined them up along the outside of the bouncy house with the other children's shoes, and jumped inside. As a mom, one of my favorite things was to see the joy on my children's faces and hear their delighted laughter as they bounced and stumbled around trying to chase one another. They looked so happy! They looked so free! When they had exhausted themselves, they climbed out and picked up their shoes, and I waited on the side to help them. As they headed over to me, however, an older White man grabbed my four-year-old son, and accused him of stealing his grandson's shoes. My maternal instinct kicked in, seeing the terror on my son's face as the man attempted to grab Cairo's shoes from him. Before I could intervene, however, the man's family took the shoes from him and handed them back to Cairo. They told him that those shoes were Cairo's, and they apologized to us.

I don't remember much after that except for the feelings of anger, frustration, confusion, and helplessness. This felt racially motivated to me, but I also wondered if the man was just confused. I hated the racial calculus I had to engage in. I hated that I couldn't just enjoy a day out with my children. My children wanted to stay and enjoy the rest of the fair, but it had been ruined for me, and I just wanted to retreat to the safety of our home.

This memory brings to mind the story Ta-Nehisi Coates (2015) writes about in *Between the World and Me* about a similar experience he had with his son:

> Perhaps you remember that time we went to see Howl's Moving Castle on the Upper West Side. You were almost five years old. The theater was crowded, and when we came out we rode a set of escalators down to the ground floor. As we came off, you were moving at the dawdling speed of a small child. A white woman pushed you and said, "Come on!" Many things now happened at once. There was the reaction of any parent when a stranger lays a hand on the body of [their] child. And there was my own insecurity in my ability to protect

your black body. And more: There was my sense that this woman was pulling rank. I knew, for instance, that she would not have pushed a black child out on my part of Flatbush, because she would be afraid there and would sense, if not know, that there would be a penalty for such an action. But I was not out on my part of Flatbush. And I was not in West Baltimore. And I was far from The Mecca. I forgot all of that. I was only aware that someone had invoked their right over the body of my son. I turned and spoke to this woman, and my words were hot with all of the moment and all of my history. She shrunk back, shocked. A white man standing nearby spoke up in her defense. I experienced this as his attempt to rescue the damsel from the beast. He had made no such attempt on behalf of my son. And he was now supported by other white people in the assembling crowd. The man came closer. He grew louder. I pushed him away. He said, "I could have you arrested!" I did not care. I told him this, and the desire to do much more was hot in my throat. This desire was only controllable because I remembered someone standing off to the side there, bearing witness to more fury than he had ever seen from me—you.

I came home shook. It was a mix of shame for having gone back to the law of the streets mixed with rage—"I could have you arrested!" Which is to say: "I could take your body."

I have told you this story many times not out of bravado but out of a need for absolution. I have never been a violent person . . . Malcolm made sense to me not out of a love of violence but because nothing in my life prepared me to understand tear gas as deliverance, as those Black History Month martyrs of the Civil Right Movement did. But more than any shame I feel about my own actual violence, my greatest regret was that in seeking to defend you I was, in fact, endangering you. (93–95)

This pulling rank that Coates illustrates reminds me of what Christian Cooper experienced in 2020 when he asked Amy Cooper (no relation) to follow the rules of the Central Park bramble and put her dog on a leash. He was in the park bird-watching. She threatened to (and did) call the police. This all occurred at around the same time as Breonna Taylor and George Floyd were murdered by the police, and I'm sure this threat evoked the same fears for Christian as Coates shares and as I experienced in front of the bouncy house.

Unfortunately, incidents like these are not unique. In May 2019, Black and Brown students from the Helen Y. Davis Leadership Academy Charter Public School in Dorchester, Massachusetts, were harassed and racially profiled during a trip to the Museum of Fine Arts. Although the museum issued an apology, the damage was already done.

With your students, you can read the Ta-Nahesi Coates excerpt, or an article about what happened to the students at the Museum of Fine Arts aloud, and then have the students record their own reflection using the following discussion prompts:

- Write about an uncomfortable situation when either you were in a place where you expected to be included, but instead were excluded, or you witnessed someone else being excluded. What happened? How did you feel? Did you tell anyone how you felt or what you saw?

- How would you have felt if you were Ta-Nahesi Coates or his son? How would you have felt if you were one of the students from Dorchester at the Museum of Fine Arts?

- If you were near the escalator when the incident happened with Ta-Nahesi Coates and his son or at the Museum of Fine Arts when the students from Dorchester were there, what do you wish you could have said to them? What do you wish you could've said to the woman who pushed Ta-Nahesi Coates's son and the man who threatened to have him arrested? What do you wish you could have said to the people who racially profiled the students from Dorchester?

You can follow up by inviting students to share their reflections with the class and then facilitate a discussion with your students to help them to build empathy. Learning about how everyday experiences like a field trip, bouncy house, or mall trip can be so different for People of Color can help your students to build empathy. It's important to note that if you have Students of Color in your class, you should not compel them to share their experiences, as that could be triggering and traumatic for a student who is the only Person of Color in a class, or one of few Students of Color.

In order for us to move beyond and heal from the pain of our past that extends into our present, there must be awareness, empathy, changed hearts and minds, and as my friend and colleague Leigh Ann Erickson of The Undone Movement shares, lament. Lament is different from shame and guilt. Shame and guilt make us want to hide, avoid, defend, deflect, and shift blame. Lament is what fueled the work of South Africa's Truth and Reconciliation Commission after the horrors of apartheid. Lament provides us with the opportunity to grieve and to reimagine a better society for all of us. Lament comes from empathy and can lead to resolve.

These stories can feel heavy for students, and for them to not feel stuck with a sense of despair, we need to show them how to build radical empathy—empathy in which we actively consider another person's point of view and in order to connect more deeply with them—and take action based on what we learn. It can't be too soon because awareness has to precede action, but we don't want to stop at having them gaze through windows without equipping students to apply what they've learned. In order for learning to really take root, students need to know that they can take part in changing some of the troubling things they'll see as they look beyond their own realities. We'll explore this more in Chapter 7.

# Breathe and Reflect

Have you ever experienced being othered? Have you ever witnessed someone being othered? Have you noticed your students othering one another? What are some ways that you have responded when your eyes have been opened to the painful experiences of people who are racially different from you? Reflect on those experiences and how you might be able to support your students to recognize and respond when they see someone experiencing an interrupted sense of belonging. ■

_____

_____

_____

_____

_____

_____

_____

_____

_____

_____

_____

_____

_____

_____

_____

_____

_____

_____

_____

_____

_____

_____

_____

# Examining Race Through Literary Analysis

Darcy Annino, Martha Santa Maria (she/her/hers), Sara Nadeau (she/her), and Eileen Sears (she/her/hers) are colleagues at the Middlebury Union Middle School in the Addison Central School District in a mostly White rural community in Middlebury, Vermont. They collaborate to create ABAR learning experiences for their middle school students in their Individuals and Societies and Language and Literature classes using *Stamped: Racism, Antiracism, and You* by Ibram X. Kendi and Jason Reynolds and *The Hate U Give* by Angie Thomas as the foundation of their work.

Prior to the start of the unit, they share a letter with families, providing a description of the content of each of the books, the connections to recent events, why they chose these books, and some of the challenging aspects of the books (see Figure 5.2). Partnering with families is a critical step when engaging in ABAR instructional practices with students. It gives families the opportunities to hear and understand the rationale behind your instructional decisions from your perspective instead of from those who have false opinions about the value of these books and whether they are worthy to be read.

These educators also developed the following community agreements with students prior to beginning the unit and shared the key words that came up in the agreement discussions:

1. We will actively listen to each other.

2. We will use "I" statements.

3. We will THINK before we speak (Is it True, Helpful, Important, Necessary, or Kind?).

4. We will create a safe space for all to participate.

5. We will respect everyone.

6. We will be willing to go outside our comfort zone and be open to new ideas.

7. We will be okay with silence.

When exploring this content, it is important to unpack the words that come up in your discussion about this content with students as well as key words, terms, and phrases you'll be engaging students with in the unit; Figure 5.3 shows a word cloud that students developed during this discussion. Figure 5.4 provides the "Language Matters" vocabulary list that Darcy, Eileen, Martha, and Sara shared with students.

FIGURE 5.2  Letter to Families

# MIDDLEBURY UNION MIDDLE SCHOOL

*Excellence through rigor, responsiveness, equity and partnerships*

_____ **Interim Principal**                    _____ **Counselor**

_____ **Interim Assistant Principal**          _____ **Counselor**

November 19, 2020

Dear Phoenix and Ohana Families:

Shortly after Thanksgiving break, your child will be embarking on an interdisciplinary unit of study in their Individuals and Societies and Language and Literature classes entitled Race and Racism in America. Within it, we will provide students with opportunities to engage in conversations and learning activities about race and racism that are sustained across two content areas, using two rich, complex texts as the foundation of our work: Stamped: Racism, Antiracism, and You by Dr. Ibram X. Kendi and Jason Reynolds and The Hate U Give by Angie Thomas. Our hope is that within the supportive environment of our classrooms, we can explore these issues through the lens of two different literary genres.

Stamped: Racism, Antiracism, and You is a nonfiction history book and is a "remix" for teen readers of Kendi's award-winning Stamped from the Beginning, which won the National Book Award in 2016. Stamped takes teen readers on an accessible journey through the history of racist ideas in America, and, as Goodreads states, "inspires hope for an antiracist future." The New York Times Book Review echoes this, writing "Reynolds's engaging, clear prose shines a light on difficult and confusing subjects. . . . This is no easy feat" (https://www.nytimes.com/2020/03/06/books/review/stamped-ibram-x-kendi-jason-reynolds.html).

The Hate U Give is a work of young adult fiction and follows a specific time in the life of a black teenager named Starr, who witnesses the shooting of her childhood friend, Khalil, at the hands of a police officer, and must make a series of difficult decisions as she figures out who she is and what she wants to stand for. This book has garnered many awards and has been highly recommended for young teen readers by countless organizations, including the American Library Association, which calls it "An inarguably important book that demands the widest possible readingership" (ala.org). It was also chosen as the 2020 Vermont Reads novel by the Vermont Council for the Humanities, whose directors write, "The powerful themes of The Hate U Give have been brought into sharper focus for millions of Americans by the murders of George Floyd, Breonna Taylor, and Ahmaud Arbury" (https://www.vermonthumanities.org/).

While this novel is held in high esteem, we do feel it is important to alert you to the fact that it contains expletives. The language is not included for gratuitous shock value or sensationalism; rather, it is simply the result of real characters living their lives in unstructured moments within "unscripted," natural interactions with one another. While we do not condone or encourage this type of language within our classrooms, we believe that the value of this text outweighs the discomfort we might initially feel at seeing some of these expletives in print. We will certainly discuss this with students before beginning the book and make certain that our expectations for interactions with one another around this issue—and other sensitive issues that The Hate U Give and Stamped highlight and illustrate—are guided by classroom norms and agreements that we have decided upon ahead of time with the students. Already, we have invited all students on both teams to anonymously share their ideas for creating norms around having difficult conversations in a Google Survey, and the results will be collated, shared with students, and used to create our list of agreements so everyone can feel safe in our classrooms, is able to learn and grow, ask hard questions, and gain a greater understanding of these complicated, timely, and important issues.

Finally, a couple of logistical notes. First, we will distribute these books to students very soon. We would like to recognize and thank the Vermont Council for the Humanities and Vermont-NEA for awarding us grants towards the purchase of some of the title copies, as well as The Vermont Book Shop for its generous discount so that we may offer these titles to all our Grade 8 students. Each student will get a borrowed copy of both texts (assigned a specific MUMS number), and we would like them to leave these books at home; we will have a class set that remains in our classroom. This way, students will not accidentally leave them at school, rendering them unable to read at home on their "remote" days. They will be expected to read each week, and both classes will supply students with a weekly reading calendar to keep them on track. Additional scaffolding will be provided to support students (e.g., key excerpts for analysis, chapter summaries, plotline, etc.) that reinforces important ideas from the reading. Both classes will keep reading journals, which will invite students to interact with Stamped and The Hate U Give in a variety of ways (e.g., art, quote analysis, summary, photography, creative writing, argument writing) and receive feedback from us throughout the unit.

It will be essential for students to keep up with their reading; any support you will be able to offer at home would be much appreciated. And on that note, we hope that this unit will inspire conversations at home. Ask your child what they are reading and learning and studying, and together, we can support students as they become more informed citizens of our world! Of course, if you have any questions, thoughts, or concerns, please feel free to contact us.

With great appreciation,

Darcy Annino, Phoenix Team Individuals and Societies

Sara Nadeau, Ohana Team Individuals and Societies

Martha Santa Maria, Ohana Team Language and Literature

Eileen Sears, Phoenix Team Language and Literature

FIGURE 5.3   Word Cloud Example Based on Student Discussion

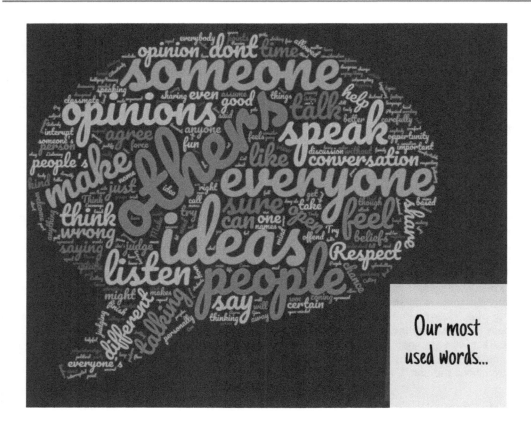

Our most used words...

Darcy, Martha, Sara, and Eileen have shared student work that builds on the book discussions and exemplifies what students are capable of when provided with learning opportunities. *The Hate U Give* virtual gallery is where students display the artwork they created as a way of exploring the themes in the book. The virtual gallery is an online slide presentation in which each slide includes a painting, drawing, poem, or other artistic work along with an audio link where students explain their art pieces. Students also created text-to-text connections presentations in response to *The Hate U Give* and *Don't Ask Me Where I'm From*.

In these presentations, students have included visual representations of their understanding of important words from the unit's word bank. They have also made connections not only to the main text but also to related content like a study about how Black drivers are more likely to be stopped by the police in Vermont as well as an article about Black parents describing the talk they give to their children about the police. Students also wrote essays in response to reading *All American Boys*,

FIGURE 5.4   Language Matters Example Vocabulary List

## Language Matters

Since we don't necessarily share a common understanding of these **words in context to this inquiry unit,** it is important to be clear as we communicate our ideas.

| | |
|---|---|
| **Activist**<br>noun | A person who believes strongly in political or social change and takes part in activities such as public protests to try to make this happen. |
| **Agency**<br>noun | Your power to make effective change. It's your ability to make choices and decisions. |
| **Ally**<br>noun | Someone who helps or stands up for someone who is being bullied or the target of prejudice. |
| **Antiracist**<br>adj. | Opposed to the unfair treatment of people who belong to other races. |
| **Assimilate**<br>verb | To take on the customs, mannerisms, and ideas of a dominant group in order to fit in.<br><br>*Assimilationist: Someone who takes on the customs, mannerisms, and ideas of a dominant culture.* |
| **Bias**<br>noun | A preference either for or against an individual or group that affects fair judgment.<br><br>**Conscious bias** involves preconceived opinions that a person is aware of, comfortable with, and/or has no intention of altering or rectifying.<br><br>**Unconscious/implicit bias** is the implicitly or unconsciously internalized perceptions about certain groups of people. |
| **Bigotry**<br>noun | Intolerant prejudice that glorifies one's own group and denigrates members of other groups. |
| **Code switching**<br>noun | The act of changing social behaviors, language, and appearance to assimilate to the norms of a dominant group. |
| **Cultural Appropriation**<br>noun | Taking of cultural elements—including symbols, art, language, customs, clothing, etc.—for one's own use or profit, often without understanding, acknowledgment, or respect for its value in the original culture. Results from the assumption of a dominant culture's right to take other cultural elements. |
| **Culture**<br>noun | A social system of meaning and custom that is developed by a group of people to assure its adaptation and survival. These groups are distinguished by a set of unspoken rules that shape values, beliefs, habits, patterns of thinking, behaviors, and styles of communication. |

*(Continued)*

(Continued)

| Discrimination<br>noun | Treating a person or particular group of people differently, especially in a worse way from the way in which you treat other people, because of their skin color, gender, sexuality, ability, religion, etc. Discrimination is an action that can come from prejudice. |
|---|---|
| Diversity<br>noun | Means different or varied. Diversity includes all the ways in which people differ, and it encompasses all the different characteristics that make one individual or group different from another. It is all-inclusive and recognizes everyone and every group as part of the diversity that should be valued. |
| Equality<br>noun | The right of different groups of people to have a similar social position and receive the same treatment. |
| Equity<br>noun | The situation in which everyone is treated fairly or justly. |
| Ethnicity<br>noun | A social construct that divides people into smaller social groups based on characteristics such as shared sense of group membership, values, behavioral patterns, language, political and economic interests, history, and ancestral geographical base. |
| Explicit<br>adj. | Communicated directly in a clear and exact way. |
| Identity<br>noun | An individual's awareness and experience of being a member of a group; the racial and ethnic categories that an individual chooses to describe themselves based on such factors as physical appearance, cultural affiliation, early socialization, and personal experience. |
| Implicit<br>adj. | Suggested but not communicated directly. |
| Inclusion<br>noun | Authentically bringing traditionally excluded individuals and/or groups into processes, activities, and decision/policy making in a way that shares power. |
| Injustice<br>noun | The condition of being unfair and lacking justice, or an action that is unfair. |
| Institutional<br>adj. | Relating to the systems and structures within an organization. |
| Intersectionality<br>adj. | The way in which different types of discrimination (unfair treatment because of a person's sex, race, etc.) are linked to and affect each other. |
| Marginalize<br>verb | Treating a person, group, or concept as secondary, unimportant, inferior, or abnormal compared with those who hold more power in society. |
| Micro-aggression<br>noun | A small act or remark that makes someone feel insulted or treated badly because of their race, sex, etc., even though the insult, etc. may not have been intended, and that can combine with other similar acts or remarks over time to cause emotional harm. |

| | |
|---|---|
| **Oppression**<br>noun | The systematic subjugation of one social group by a more powerful social group for the social, economic, and political benefit of the more powerful social group.<br><br>Oppression = Power + Prejudice |
| **Perspective**<br>noun | A particular way of viewing things that depends on one's experience and personality. |
| **Power**<br>noun | The ability to influence others and impose one's beliefs. Power is not only in an individual relationship but also a cultural one. |
| **Prejudice**<br>noun | A pre-judgment or unjustifiable, and usually negative, attitude of one type of individual or groups toward another identity group (race, religion, gender, etc.) and its members. Such negative attitudes are typically based on unsupported generalizations (or stereotypes) that deny the right of individual members of certain groups to be recognized and treated as individuals with individual characteristics. Prejudices are learned and can be unlearned. |
| **Privilege**<br>noun | Unearned social power/access/benefits a person gets just by belonging to a dominant social group. |
| **Race**<br>noun | A made-up social construct, and not an actual biological fact to support worldviews that viewed some groups of people as superior and some as inferior. Race designations have changed over time. |
| **Racism**<br>noun | When a person or group of people with power is/are able to act on their racial prejudice in a harmful way. *Racism is related to but different from racial prejudice.*<br><br>Prejudice + Power = Racism |
| **Segregation**<br>noun | The practice of keeping people of different races, religions, etc., separate from each other. |
| **Stereotype**<br>noun | The false idea that all members of a group are the same and think and behave in the same way.<br><br>Often a distorted view of a person/group that is not based on any fact. |
| **Systematic**<br>adj. | Done in a methodical and planned way. |
| **Systemic**<br>adj. | Relating to or affecting the whole of a system, organization, etc. rather than just some parts of it. |
| **Truth**<br>noun | The body of real things, events, and facts.<br><br>Truth is something that squares with reality. |
| **White Supremacy**<br>noun | The idea (ideology) that White people and the ideas, thoughts, beliefs, and actions of White people are superior to People of Color and their ideas, thoughts, beliefs, and actions.<br><br>The social, economic, and political systems that collectively enable White people to maintain power over people of other races. |

*American Born Chinese, The Hate U Give,* and *Stamped: Racism, Antiracism, and You.* You can access the virtual gallery and text-to-text connections in the online companion to this book: resources.corwin.com/openwindows.

By engaging in reading and discussing contributions, histories, and experiences that differ from their own, students have the opportunity to deepen their understanding of the larger human experience and build the schema needed for continuing this learning.

# Breathe and Reflect

Use this space to reflect on when you've successfully collaborated with colleagues and what you notice and wonder about the outcomes of Darcy, Martha, Sara, and Eileen's collaboration. ▪

_____

_____

_____

_____

_____

_____

_____

_____

_____

_____

_____

_____

_____

_____

_____

_____

_____

_____

_____

_____

_____

_____

_____

_____

_____

_____

_____

_____

# Exploring Challenges Through Interactive Read Alouds

Sarah Halter Hahesy uses interactive read alouds and picture books like *A Pig Is Moving In* by Claudia Fries to help her third-grade students develop an understanding of terms like *stereotype, prejudice, ally, discriminate, oppression, systems of advantage* and *disadvantage.* You'll find a list of titles appropriate for interactive read alouds in the online companion: resources.corwin.com/openwindows.

Here are the questions Sarah engages her students in before and during reading *A Pig Is Moving In*; these can be adapted for any read aloud:

- Before reading
  - What do you think about when you think of pigs? This will lay the foundation for unpacking the concept of *stereotyping*.
  - Based on your thoughts about pigs, predict how other animals will feel about the pig. This will open the door to talking about the concept of *prejudice* and to prepare students for how it can look to be an *ally*.

- During reading
  - After Doctor Fox complains to Henrietta Hen about the pig, ask students to say how Doctor Fox's stereotype of the pig turned into prejudice. This can lead to discussing the word *discriminate*.
  - How does prejudice cause the other animals to discriminate against the pig? How could they have been an ally instead?

- After reading
  - What can we do to be kind and welcoming to other people? How can we be allies to others who might be different from us?

Think of books you read with your students and ways you could engage your students similarly with an interactive read aloud. If you work together with colleagues, you can create and share questions based on a variety of books with one another. As much as possible, try to collaborate on this work.

You can also incorporate interactive read alouds that both teach specific literacy skills and model for students what it looks like for people of various backgrounds to develop a positive identity at all levels. Elementary and secondary students would appreciate these books, which can be quick openers to deeper conversation and analysis. To provide more windows for students, you can intentionally choose books written by and about people who students may not typically have the benefit of knowing personally and who they may have misperceptions of based on prevalent inaccurate or absent narratives. The online companion contains an annotated list of books for elementary students and one for middle and high school students to get you started (see resources.corwin.com/open windows).

https://bit.ly/3xOiHye

It is also critical that students don't have a myopic view of any particular group of people. This is an important consideration, especially when it comes to addressing topics like enslavement, internment, genocide/displacement, discrimination, and civil rights. These are important stories to tell, and at the same time, as Chimamanda Ngozi Adichie shares in her 2009 TED Talk, we have to be aware of "The Danger of a Single Story."

As much as it's important to share accurate history with students, we must also make sure they understand the complexity of all of our identities—the struggle but also the joy, accomplishments, resilience, strength, and celebration. It is imperative for students to learn that no one's life is solely about struggle. Humans are so much more than the challenges we face. You can build on the foundation you laid in Chapter 3 as students explored the different parts of their identities to show that the same is true for all groups of people.

Jill Ferraresso (she/her/hers), who teaches second grade at the Atrium School in Watertown, Massachusetts, supports her students with perspective-taking by engaging them in an Upstander project. Students choose an upstander to study whom they will impersonate at the end of the year after engaging in a deep semester-long study about the person. Jill tries to include upstanders from as many different backgrounds as she can, so the list of people they can study includes people like Jackie Robinson, Frederick Douglass, Malala Yousafzai, Frida Kahlo, Langston Hughes, Malcolm X, and Dr. King.

The way Jill approaches this work with her students is important to consider—as we're thinking about the perspectives of people we don't often learn about, students can learn how layered we all are as people. Even when we have accomplished notable things, we are not only the sum total of the notable things we've done. Harriet Tubman was more than a conductor on the Underground Railroad. Rosa Parks was more than someone who refused to give up her seat on a bus. We are also not the sum total of the mistakes we've made. We are more. This is important to remember, because though we identify some people as upstanders, they are not perfect. None of us is. That's the beauty of being an upstander. You don't have to be perfect to work toward a more fair, just world for everyone. You have to be willing to try, make mistakes, learn, and keep going.

# Breathe and Reflect

What are some picture or chapter books or texts you have used or might use with your students to help them to build a positive identity for themselves and to engage in authentic learning from and about people who may differ from them? ■

_____

_____

_____

_____

_____

_____

_____

_____

_____

_____

_____

_____

_____

_____

_____

_____

_____

_____

_____

_____

_____

_____

_____

_____

_____

At any grade level, we can also implement picture books that help students to see how they and other students can appreciate the different shades of our skin and textures of our hair. This is especially important when we consider how Black children's hair has been penalized in our school spaces. I think many of us may remember the image of Andrew Johnson having his locs cut during a wrestling match in 2019. You can help White students to reflect on how it feels to have, or to have someone in their family, with physical features that may be unique in their family or school community. This can include freckles, curls, hair length, height, weight, gender expression (e.g., girls who enjoy playing football or boys who enjoy playing with dolls), and body differences. This will prepare them to relate to/connect with the content of these stories about hair and skin tone and texture. The online companion provides an annotated bibliography of some great picture books to get you started (resources.corwin.com/openwindows).

# Breathe and Reflect

What narratives have you been exposed to about the hair and skin of people who are racially different from you? What narratives have your students been exposed to? How can you use literature to help them reimagine how they think about the physical features of people who are racially different from them? How can you do this in a way that does not single out Students of Color who may be in your class? ■

_____

_____

_____

_____

_____

_____

_____

_____

_____

_____

_____

_____

_____

_____

_____

_____

_____

_____

_____

_____

_____

_____

_____

_____

_____

_____

## SHARING BOOK REFLECTIONS

One of the ways you can ensure that students are not only enjoying and learning from stories featuring people who differ from them but that they're also allowing the messages of those stories to change the way they think and what they believe about other people is by encouraging students to write reflections about the books you're reading with them as well as books they're reading independently from your inclusive classroom library. In a reading reflection, students summarize the story then reflect on the impact the book had on them.

You can create your own model of a reading reflection as an example for your students based on the literature you're exploring with them and then support them to select a book to write about. Figure 5.5 provides a glimpse at Emily's book reflection about Jacqueline Woodson's *The Other Side*—a story about how Clover and Annie creatively countered segregation in their town; Emily is a fourth grader.

---

FIGURE 5.5   Emily's Book Reflection (Fourth Grade)

---

The story, *The Other Side*, by Jacqueline Woodson, is about two little girls named Clover and Annie. They live on separate sides of a fence. The time of the story is during segregation when two different races (Black and White) were set apart because of their skin colors. The girls, Annie and Clover, are curious about each other, but there is a fence between them. The fence separates them because of their skin color. This is why the fence is very important to the story. It expresses without words the separation and the time of segregation.

What would you do if there was something in the way of your friendship?

---

# Breathe and Reflect

Think about a time you have connected meaningfully with someone across racial differences. Use the space below to reflect on Emily's question: What would you do if there was something in the way of your friendship? If you have not had this experience, why do you think that is? ∎

_____

_____

_____

_____

_____

_____

_____

_____

_____

_____

_____

_____

_____

_____

_____

_____

_____

_____

_____

_____

_____

_____

_____

_____

When we keep in mind that young children can—and want to—read books and talk about experiences other than what's familiar, we can find ways into conversation and learning using picture books. Kara Pranikoff (she/her) is a second-grade teacher at P.S. 234, a mostly White public school in Manhattan, New York City. This public elementary school is known throughout the region for its academic rigor, inquiry-based learning, and integrative social studies curricula. Kara's book *Teaching Talk: A Practical Guide to Fostering Student Thinking and Conversation* (Pranikoff 2017) shares ways to foster productive and independent student discussions in elementary classrooms. Throughout her years as an educator, Kara has worked to foster strong communication at every age and believes schools can be a space where all topics can be discussed. She brings ABAR teaching to the communities she learns with, most pointedly her second graders who are ready to think about the largest issues and are moving forward with open eyes and strong voices. Kara encourages the second graders in her care to be changemakers and the guiding principles of being a changemaker include:

FIGURE 5.6   Example of Student Reflections on ABAR Lessons

- **Loving engagement:** We need to engage with all people in a fair and peaceful way. We need to treat everyone with love.

- **Collective value:** Everybody is important and has the right to be safe and happy, no matter what they believe, where they are from, or who they love.

- **Empathy:** It's important to think about how other people feel. You can think about how you would feel if the same thing happened to you.

- **Diversity:** Different people do different things and have different feelings. It's important that we have lots of different kinds of people in our community and that everyone feels safe.

Figure 5.6 shows the entrance to Kara's classroom. You can see how even young children can embrace ABAR ways of being when guided in the journey. Picture books can be an important first step on that journey.

# Breathe and Reflect

Use this space to reflect on what you notice and wonder about Kara's changemaker concepts of loving engagement, collective value, empathy, and diversity. Are there instructional moves that you might use to inspire your own ABAR work with your students? ■

_____

_____

_____

_____

_____

_____

_____

_____

_____

_____

_____

_____

_____

_____

_____

_____

_____

_____

_____

_____

_____

_____

_____

_____

_____

_____

_____

_____

# Parallel Tracks for Teachers and Students

Opening windows onto ABAR thinking and being is an ongoing process for adults and students alike. Fortunately, there are many books now about the history of race in the United States that offer young adult versions. If you and a group of colleagues can read and discuss the adult version of some of the following books, you can create opportunities for your students to read the young adult versions alongside adults and for the groups to discuss what they're learning with one another. If there are students' family members who are interested in extending their learning about race, they can read the adult versions as a group and will then be better equipped to support their children as they're engaging with the books.

| FOR TEACHERS | FOR STUDENTS |
|---|---|
| *A People's History of the United States* by Howard Zinn | *A Young People's History of the United States* by Howard Zinn |
| *An Indigenous Peoples' History of the United States* by Roxanne Dunbar-Ortiz | *An Indigenous Peoples' History of the United States for Young People* by Roxanne Dunbar-Ortiz |
| *Just Mercy: A Story of Justice and Redemption* by Bryan Stevenson | *Just Mercy (Adapted for Young Adults): A True Story of the Fight for Justice* by Bryan Stevenson |
| *One Person, No Vote: How Voter Suppression Is Destroying Our Democracy* by Carol Anderson | *One Person, No Vote (YA Edition): How Not All Voters Are Treated Equally* by Carol Anderson |
| *The Burning: Black Wall Street and the Tulsa Race Massacre of 1921* by Tim Madigan | *The Burning (Young Readers Edition): Black Wall Street and the Tulsa Race Massacre of 1921* by Tim Madigan and adapted for young people by Hilary Beard |
| *Stamped From the Beginning* by Ibram X. Kendi | *Stamped: Racism, Antiracism, and You (A Remix of the National Book Award–Winning Stamped From the Beginning)* by Jason Reynolds and Ibram X. Kendi

*Stamped (For Kids): Racism, Antiracism, and You* by Jason Reynolds and Ibram X. Kendi and adapted by Sonja Cherry-Paul |
| *White Rage* by Carol Anderson | *We Are Not Yet Equal: Understanding Our Racial Divide* by Carol Anderson |

In this chapter, we have reflected on the importance of equipping ourselves with the ABAR instructional skills that many of us didn't receive in our teacher preparation programs, and we have explored some of the instructional moves and resources we can implement with our students to open windows that will expand their understanding of our world. In Chapter 6, we'll learn how to help students build on that understanding and examine other perspectives through critical discourse.

# Opening Windows Into Overlooked Perspectives

## Building Skills Through Discourse

On February 23, 2020, Ahmaud Arbery, a twenty-five-year-old Black man, was pursued and fatally shot by White residents in Brunswick, Georgia, while he was jogging through the neighborhood. On March 13, 2020, Breonna Taylor, a twenty-six-year-old Black woman, was shot and killed by police in her Louisville, Kentucky, apartment. On May 25, 2020, George Floyd, a forty-six-year-old Black man, was murdered outside of a convenience store in Minneapolis, Minnesota, by police officer Derek Chauvin. Chauvin kneeled on George Floyd's neck for nine minutes and twenty-nine seconds. The circumstances surrounding these three murders launched protests that expanded beyond the United States, even in the midst of a global pandemic. Many companies and organizations put out Black Lives Matter statements and put up black squares on their social media feeds to make a public statement of solidarity against the killing of unarmed Black people. Some teachers engaged their students in the learning experiences that are part of the Black Lives Matter at School Week of Action (https://www.BlackLives MatteratSchool.com).

In light of this raised awareness regarding experiences with racial injustice, current and former Black students at some private schools around the United States began to tell stories of the biased treatment and microaggressions they've experienced in their learning spaces with *Black at (name of the school)* Instagram accounts (e.g., @BlackatBCHigh, @BlackatExeter, @BlackatWoodward, @BlackatSidwell-Friends), and administrators, teachers, community members, and other students at the schools became more aware of the perspectives of Black students. Meanwhile, students at some schools responded with *Woke at (name of the school)* accounts led by self-described concerned community members to allegedly "support free speech and open discourse, and to seek truth in education without leftist indoctrination"; these accounts stem from the same mindset as those who are attacking what they're referring to as critical race theory instead of being genuinely curious about perspectives that differ from their own.

What would happen, if, instead of defaulting to responding defensively to ideas that are unfamiliar and new to them, students who typically experience privilege learned to tap into their lost sense of curiosity and wonder? What if they asked more questions instead of making uninformed and misinformed statements?

This chapter will explore the benefits of teaching students how to engage in discourse. In addition to developing research, teamwork, and analytical skills, learning to engage in discourse also helps students to understand the importance of developing fact-based, compelling, rational, reasoned arguments to support purposeful discussion and dialogue.

By incorporating effective practices, you will learn to effectively help students to integrate their developing knowledge of the likely unknown perspectives of people from marginalized groups and White people who worked/are working in solidarity with Black, Indigenous, and People of Color (BIPOC) as well as to lay the foundation for solving societal challenges.

## Addressing the Underlying Causes of Injustice

Bryan Stevenson, a lawyer, social justice activist, founder and executive director of the Equal Justice Institute, and author of *Just Mercy*, offers an important perspective about how to address the underlying causes of racial prejudice and injustice. Stevenson believes that there are four ways to fight against injustice:

- Get proximate to the issues.

- Change the narrative that people are different based on skin color.

- Fight against hopelessness.

- Get uncomfortable. (Varela 2016)

Discussing the ills of the past and their connection to today will help us to engage in the truth and reconciliation needed to effectively address present manifestations of racial injustice. Other countries have benefitted from this approach— South Africa after apartheid and Rwanda after the genocide. In the United States, however, we don't yet embrace proximity or genuinely explore the foundations of the issues we face nor take the time to reflect on the harm that is being done to all of us when we are not proximate to one another.

We live in physically hypersegregated communities, and we create digital segregation as well. Our social media feeds can be filled with Facebook feuds and Twitter wars, people taking sides instead of digging into the root problem to find a solution. When the immigration debate during Trump's presidency manifested in a Facebook post about the horrors of kids in cages, for example, someone else posted that Obama also put kids in cages—yet there's no discussion of how to create and sustain just and humane immigration policies. When we don't like what we read or see online, we unfriend, unfollow, and block people and then retreat to our echo chambers where we can be surrounded by those who are like-minded. We don't know how to engage in meaningful discussions where we can move beyond uninformed opinions and grapple with facts, evidence, and perspectives that differ from our own toward a perspective that honors the human dignity of all people.

While it's natural to focus on what we disagree with, we can't end there. We need to learn how to collaborate to find solutions to our challenges. As I learned from James E. Ford, MAT, executive director of the Center for Racial Equity in Education (CREED) at the 2018 National Network of State Teachers of the Year (NNSTOY) Conference, we can't focus so much on what we want to tear down that we forget to think about what we want to build. Students can develop these skills through discourse.

When I talk about grappling with perspectives that differ from our own, I want to be clear that the dignity and rights of any person or group is never up for debate. This is why I'm using the frame of discourse as we explore how debating skills and experiences can help students with perspective taking, idea development, and problem-solving. If someone's beliefs are bigoted, xenophobic, racist, hurtful, harmful, or exclusionary, I am not suggesting that there is space to agree to disagree. (Refer to Chapter 4 for suggestions for disarming or redirecting harmful statements in class or in dialogue with other adults.)

There is space, however, for discourse and debate about the ideas at the foundation of *how* we dismantle injustices. This is the type of discourse we foster in an antiracist classroom. We see this exemplified in the differences between Booker T. Washington and W. E. B. Du Bois with regard to the advancement of Black people in the United States, as well as Malcolm X's and Martin Luther King Jr.'s approaches to civil rights. Our common belief must be that the injustices need to be dismantled and that through discourse we seek solutions, not blame or excuses.

*Crash Course Black American History* videos are a great resource for learning about unknown history and perspectives. Clint Smith is the host, and Episode 22 focuses on Booker T. Washington and W. E. B. Du Bois. You can find a link to a list of *Crash Course Black American History* videos in the online companion to this book.

https://bit.ly/3ESA0Qp

# Breathe and Reflect

Use this space to reflect on a way you've intentionally ventured (or would like to venture) beyond racially segregated spaces to increase your proximity to racially marginalized and excluded people. How did this experience help you to shift racial narratives? How did you benefit personally from this increased proximity? ■

_____

_____

_____

_____

_____

_____

_____

_____

_____

_____

_____

_____

_____

_____

_____

_____

_____

_____

_____

_____

_____

_____

_____

_____

# Benefits of Debate/Discourse

Engaging in discourse by learning foundational debating skills has benefits that extend beyond perspective taking. According to the American Debate League, debating can help to develop the following skills:

- Oral and written communication skills

- Critical thinking skills

- Research, organization, and presentation skills (American Debate League 2022)

Students can develop:

- Questions

- Abstract and analytical thinking skills

- Problem-solving skills

- Point of view

- Ethics

- Teamwork and collaboration

- The ability to:
  - Distinguish fact from opinion
  - Identify bias
  - Persuade
  - Use evidence
  - Communicate conclusions
  - Take informed action

These are all skills that are outlined in the speaking and listening standards that many states use as well as the C3 Framework for Social Studies State Standards and are skills that students can build through discourse. This foundation can lead to students becoming engaged citizens.

Learning to debate ideas effectively can help students to transition from recalling facts and basic concepts and explaining ideas, which are the lowest levels of Bloom's Taxonomy, to drawing connections among ideas and justifying a stand or decision at the higher levels. You can increase the rigor of learning experiences for students through debate according to Webb's Depth of Knowledge levels as students shift from reproduction and recall (Level 1) to strategic and extended thinking (Levels 3 and 4).

## Breathe and Reflect

What are some strategies you're already implementing with your students that you can use to help students build their discourse skills? Use this space to also reflect on how you can help your students to consider perspectives they may not be aware of. ■

_____

_____

_____

_____

_____

_____

_____

_____

_____

_____

_____

_____

_____

_____

_____

_____

_____

_____

_____

_____

_____

_____

_____

_____

_____

# Having Clear Outcomes, Assessing Growth, and Monitoring Progress

In supporting White students to open more windows through discourse, it is essential that you have clear outcomes in mind before engaging in this work. We want students to

- think critically about issues and topics related to people from marginalized groups and the parts of their own racial identity they don't usually explore;

- analyze false narratives about people from groups who are racially different;

- make informed decisions as a citizen;

- move from a fixed mindset about their ability to develop this understanding to a growth mindset where they know that with effort, they can develop informed, empathetic perspectives based on facts and the lived experiences of others; and

- continue developing an awareness of self, awareness of others, awareness of social issues, and an ability to see one's potential to make societal changes.

In order to determine whether students' understanding of the issues has shifted, teachers will need to assess students' understanding of the issues prior to and following the foundational strategy instruction as well as the debate experiences. An assessment tool can be developed using the relevant C3 standard, individual state English language arts, and/or Learning for Justice standards as both a pre- and post-assessment. You can also embed formative assessment and checks for understanding throughout the experience.

https://bit.ly/3xU5qnE

Figure 6.1 provides a sample of a pre- and post-assessment you could administer for students prior to and following a discourse experience depending on what content you are engaging students with and which skills you would like students to develop.

In order to effectively assess students, you will need to have a clear understanding of what it means for a student to begin, approach, meet, and exceed expectations before engaging the students with the content and skills. For example, looking at the tool in Figure 6.1, a *beginner* engages in research, develops the ability to evaluate sources at the *approaching* level, *meets* expectations by learning to cite appropriate resources as they take a position, and *exemplifies* the skill when they can effectively use evidence to support a position. This information will inform your next instructional steps.

FIGURE 6.1 Sample of a Pre- and Post-Assessment

Student Name: _____          Date: _____

Pre- or Post-Assessment: _____

| | BEGINNING | APPROACHING | MEETING | EXCEEDING |
|---|---|---|---|---|
| The student is able to research topics, evaluate sources, take a position, and use evidence to support the position (C3 Framework). | | | | |
| The student can participate in collaborative conversations with diverse partners, including asking and answering questions (General literacy standards for speaking and listening [varies by state]). | | | | |
| The student can recognize stereotypes and relate to people as individuals rather than as representatives of groups (Social Justice Standards: Justice Domain) | | | | |
| The student can identify events relevant to the history of social justice in the United States (Social Justice Standards: Justice Domain). | | | | |
| The student can recognize that power and privilege influence relationships on institutional levels and consider how they have been affected by those dynamics (Social Justice Standards: Justice Domain). | | | | |

Additionally, it's important for students to understand how they're progressing with both skills and content. You can modify this assessment to provide students with the opportunity to engage in self-assessment of the skill and the level of skill the student has attained (e.g., *I am beginning to recognize injustice at the institutional level* or *I am approaching the ability to analyze the harmful impact of bias and discrimination*). Having this information will provide students with clarity regarding what they have accomplished and help them to set learning goals for themselves.

# Breathe and Reflect

How can you implement pre- and post-assessments as well as student self-assessments as you help students build discourse skills? How can pre- and post-assessments and student self-assessments support your antibias, antiracist (ABAR) instructional practices? ▪

_____

_____

_____

_____

_____

_____

_____

_____

_____

_____

_____

_____

_____

_____

_____

_____

_____

_____

_____

_____

_____

_____

_____

_____

_____

_____

_____

_____

# DEVELOPING FOUNDATIONAL DISCOURSE SKILLS

Debating involves students or teams arguing for the affirmative or the negative. Students arguing for the affirmative side of a debate must stay relevant to the resolution (e.g., *Resolved: The illegal use of drugs should be treated as a matter of public health, not of criminal justice*), indict the status quo, and offer a proposal designed to solve the problems identified when indicting the status quo. Students arguing for the negative side in a debate must cite the disadvantages of the affirmative case, offer counterproposals, and give critiques of the affirmative side's assumptions. Students can do this by engaging in four-step refutation:

1. *Restate* (identify the claim they are answering).

2. *Refute* (state the counterargument).

3. *Support* (offer evidence to enforce the counterargument).

4. *Conclude* (compare their refutation to their opponent's argument and show that their argument is better).

Keep in mind that the intended outcome in a debate centered around antiracist issues is to debate types of solutions, not whether or not a solution is warranted. We must begin from a place of seeking a solution and not adopting the blame orientation that is indicative of the reintegration status of White identity development.

https://bit.ly/3K7tp5i

For elementary and early secondary students, you can implement resources like the Strategic Educational Research Partnership units. This free resource includes interdisciplinary units for upper elementary and middle school educators (particularly WordGen Elementary, WordGen Weekly, and Social Studies Generation units) that help students to apply content learning to concepts like fairness, belonging, inclusion, conflict, power, resolving differences, and improving communities through word study, readers theater, debate, and writing.

Developing a sound argument involves researching the topic using reliable resources, so it will be imperative for you to provide students with ample time and opportunities to explore the facts, content, and vocabulary. Upper middle school and high school aged students can engage with more advanced issues related to the following potential debate resolutions. Let's look at a selection of potential debate topics and some of the requisite background knowledge needed:

- *The US government should change the way schools are funded to make them more equitable.*
  - Students would need to understand how schools are funded.

- *The US Department of Housing and Urban Development should take steps to reverse the impact of housing discrimination.*
  - Students would need to understand housing discrimination.

- *The US Department of Agriculture should implement strategies that eliminate food deserts.*
  - Students would need to learn about food deserts.

- *The US Department of Education should require all public school students to learn about Black history.*
  - Students would need to know what is currently included in learning standards about Black history.

- *In order to address mass incarceration, Congress should limit how much companies can profit from prisons.*
  - Students would need to know why people are arrested, what mass incarceration is, if it's fair, and how some companies profit from it.

- *In order to address mass incarceration, Congress should remove incentives for drug arrests.*
  - Students would need to understand what incentives exist for drug arrests.

- *The United States should institute reconciliation practices to address the aftermath of enslavement.*
  - Students would need to consider what all people need to be free (food, shelter, clothes, income, safety) and understand what provisions were made or not made for those who were enslaved.

- *The US government should take steps to address gerrymandering.*
  - Students would need to understand what gerrymandering is, why some people engage in it, if it's fair, and how to make sure voting access is fair.

## EXPLORING DEBATE EXAMPLES

Whenever developing a new skill, it is important to see models of effective practice and to analyze what makes those models exemplary. If students engage in the Zinn Education Project's "The Election of 1860 Role Play," for example, they will become familiar with some of the issues—namely enslavement in the South and in territories, support for homesteads, tariffs on manufactured goods, and the building of the transcontinental railroad. Teachers can build on this background knowledge by studying the Lincoln-Douglas series of debates in 1858, where Abraham Lincoln and Stephen Douglas focused on enslavement in the United States as they campaigned for an Illinois Senate seat.

Since one of the key aims of this book is to expose White students to people and content that they may not necessarily encounter, another model to share with students is the James Baldwin and Malcolm X debate from April 1961 where they discuss the nature of racism in the United States, the effectiveness of sit-ins, and possible solutions. They can listen to the debate and read the debate transcript on the Democracy Now! website. You can find the links to these debate examples in the online companion to this book.

Watching excerpts of *The Great Debaters* movie with students can also both provide them with a model of what debating can look like in action and introduce them to the story of how students on the debate team at Wiley College, a historically Black college in East Texas, triumphed over the University of Southern California's debate team in 1935—a time in the United States when segregation, discrimination, and racial violence were prevalent. Though the film alters some of the facts of this historic event, there are key aspects of the film that can help students to develop an understanding of what it looks like to debate about complex issues. For example, in the film, the debaters argued in the affirmative in support of the resolutions: *Negroes should be admitted to state universities* and *civil disobedience is a moral weapon in the fight for justice.*

# Breathe and Reflect

What are some topics you will explore prior to exploring them with your students through discourse? What are some challenges you anticipate with implementing discourse in your classroom? How can you address those challenges? ▪

_____

_____

_____

_____

_____

_____

_____

_____

_____

_____

_____

_____

_____

_____

_____

_____

_____

_____

_____

_____

_____

_____

_____

_____

_____

_____

_____

# STRATEGIES TO DEVELOP A SHARED UNDERSTANDING OF MULTIPLE PERSPECTIVES ON AN ISSUE

By incorporating ABAR practices using strategies like jigsaw, Socratic seminar, concentric/inside-outside circles, fishbowl, Visual Thinking Strategies (VTS), and four corners, you can learn to effectively engage students in becoming more aware of the unknown perspectives of people who have been historically excluded. Helping students to develop a shared understanding of unknown perspectives on various issues, providing them with opportunities to practice using evidence and examples to defend a position and integrating technology into their exploration of race-related issues provides teachers with the opportunity to learn to effectively help students to integrate their developing knowledge of the perspectives and experiences of marginalized groups and to lay the foundation for solving societal challenges.

In order for students to effectively debate an issue, they will need an understanding of the multiple perspectives on that issue. The focus should be on multiple approaches to addressing an issue versus debate over the validity of an issue. We are not debating, for example, that mass incarceration needs to be addressed. We are supporting students to think of multiple solutions. It is also important for students to learn collaboratively. Students can learn about topics using the following strategies:

## JIGSAW

Jigsaw discussions provide students with opportunities to deepen their understanding of a topic. Teachers identify multiple articles about different aspects of a particular topic and divide students into groups. There are as many students in a group as there are articles. Each student in a group reads a different article and is responsible for sharing what they learned from their assigned article with the group. Signing up for a free resource like Newsela,

https://bit.ly/3xMVHPZ

if you don't already have an account, would be ideal because it provides articles about a variety of topics at various reading levels so that all learners can access the content (https://newsela.com).

### What It Can Look Like in Action

If you want students to learn more about affirmative action in preparation for debating about equitable school funding, you can assign the following articles on Newsela at appropriate reading levels (links in the online companion):

- "Judge Rules in Harvard's Favor in Federal Affirmative Action Case"

- "College Admissions Scandal a Reminder of Injustice in America"

- "Trump Revokes Obama's Race-Based College Admissions Guidance"

This research can lead to discussions about the nature of affirmative action—who benefits from affirmative action policies and why race-based affirmative action policies are viewed differently from legacy admissions and athletic scholarships in colleges.

*Note:* These can be challenging conversations, and it will be important to revisit the guidelines in Chapter 4 with regard to creating a brave space for critical classroom conversations, particularly preparing for critical conversations, co-creating classroom agreements, and agreeing about how to disagree.

## SOCRATIC SEMINAR

The point of a Socratic seminar is not to assert opinions or prove an argument. The purpose is to practice listening, making meaning, and finding common ground. Students can build their skills with clarifying, agreeing and disagreeing, comparing and contrasting, and exploring counterexamples as well as cause and effect, benefits and burdens, point of view, perspective, and concepts like structure and function.

https://bit.ly/3k70ELH

Teachers select a text for students to explore, give students time to prepare, and determine agreements about how to engage in the seminar (e.g., monitor your airtime, ask questions about the text, clarify questions of other participants, and use evidence from the text to support ideas). The seminar begins with an open-ended question related to the text and continues through a discussion cycle following the established agreements. The seminar should conclude with an opportunity to debrief, reflect, and evaluate the experience.

### *What It Can Look Like in Action*

In 2015, Bree Newsome, a Black woman, climbed to the top of the flagpole in front of South Carolina's State House and removed the Confederate flag. While she was on the flagpole, police threatened to tase the flagpole to remove her, which would have caused significant harm to her body—and possibly her life. James Tyson, a White man, and her co-conspirator, positioned his body against the flagpole so that if the officers tased the flagpole, his body would absorb some of the shock. He knew that officers would be more hesitant to appear in the news causing harm to a White man. He used his privilege in support of justice (Helms 2015). Students can read about Bree Newsome and James Tyson and discuss what it means to work together for justice in a Socratic seminar.

## CONCENTRIC/INSIDE-OUTSIDE CIRCLES

In the concentric circles strategy, students explore ideas with a variety of classmates with one group of students composing the inside circle and another group of students composing the outside circle. The circles alternatively shift left or right so that students have the opportunity to engage in paired discussions with several classmates to share their thoughts and ideas about a topic. Concentric circles provide students with the opportunity to partner as they further develop their speaking and active listening skills. As with all strategies, teachers should debrief the experience with students at the end of the experience.

https://bit.ly/38ckxy8

### What It Can Look Like in Action

A teacher can begin by having students read one of the following Learning for Justice articles/resources (linked in the online companion):

- "Ten Myths About Immigration"

- "The Human Face of Immigration"

- "Exploring Young Immigrant Stories"

Students can then launch the circles with the following statement: *We are a nation of immigrants.* Students will begin by discussing their response to this statement and why they feel the way they do, making reference to what they learned from the article(s). Some students may have parents, family members, and/or ancestors who are immigrants, and some may be immigrants themselves, so they'll be able to speak from their lived experiences. Ideally, some students may wonder how this statement impacts Indigenous People who have experienced genocide and Black Americans whose ancestors were abducted and forced into enslavement in the United States. The teacher can ask the essential questions from the "Exploring Young Immigrant Stories" lesson plan or follow-up questions related to immigration for each rotation of the circle:

- Why do people immigrate to other countries?

- Are immigrants from all countries treated the same in the United States?

- Do you think that immigrants are treated well in most countries?

- Should immigrants be required to learn the local language?

- To what extent has the culture of your community become richer because of immigrants?

## FISHBOWL

To facilitate a fishbowl discussion, teachers select a topic for students to discuss and separate the class into students who will be inside the fishbowl asking each other questions and sharing their opinions with one another related to the topic and the group of students who will sit outside of the fishbowl as observers. It's important for the teacher to establish community agreements and rules for the discussion and to debrief the discussion when it's over—how the students think it went and what they learned from one another.

https://bit.ly/3vFA9lV

### What It Can Look Like in Action

The teacher can share the following statement with students: *The Pledge of Allegiance should be recited in school each day.* In preparation for the fishbowl discussion, you can sign up for free access to Newsela (https://newsela.com), and students can read these Newsela articles to explore different perspectives, experiences, and responses related to the Pledge of Allegiance and the national anthem (linked in the online companion):

- "NFL Owners Say Players Must Stand for the National Anthem on the Field"

- "Colin Kaepernick's New 'Just Do It' Nike Ad Pressures NFL to Take a Stand"

- "Kaepernick Wins *Sports Illustrated* Award for Protesting Injustice"

- "Black Student Sits Out the Pledge, Challenges State Law in Texas"

This discussion can branch into discussions about First Amendment rights, freedom, patriotism, and protest.

# Breathe and Reflect

Use this space to envision what it might look like to implement the jigsaw, Socratic seminar, concentric/inside-outside circles, and/or fishbowl strategies with your students as they explore typically unknown perspectives. ∎

_____

_____

_____

_____

_____

_____

_____

_____

_____

_____

_____

_____

_____

_____

_____

_____

_____

_____

_____

_____

_____

_____

_____

_____

_____

_____

_____

_____

# STRATEGIES TO PRACTICE USING EVIDENCE AND EXAMPLES TO DEFEND A POSITION

## VISUAL THINKING STRATEGIES

When I taught fifth-grade English language arts at a school in Boston, our school had a partnership with the Isabella Stewart Gardner Museum. Four times during the school year, a docent from the museum came to meet with students prior to a visit to the museum. Students had the opportunity to view and discuss pieces of artwork. When we subsequently visited the museum, the docent engaged the students with VTS. This approach accomplishes the following:

- Uses art to develop critical thinking, communication, and visual literacy skills

- Engages learners in a rigorous process of examination and meaning-making through visual art

- Measurably increases observation skills, evidential reasoning, and speculative abilities

- Engenders the willingness and ability to find multiple solutions to complex problems

- Uses facilitated discussion to enable students to practice respectful, democratic, collaborative problem-solving skills (Simmons 2019)

This included answering the following questions about various pieces of art:

- *What's going on in this picture?*

- *What do you see that makes you say that?*

- *What more can you find?*

You can use the VTS approach to analyze photographs of events and support students to notice and wonder about what they see. For example, a photograph of a student wearing a *Make America Great Again* hat from a high school in Kentucky standing in front of a Native American elder at the Lincoln Memorial while on a field trip with his school went viral in January 2019. A teacher could show students this photo, pose the VTS questions to students, and transition to a research-based discussion about whether or not it should be permissible for students to wear clothing with political statements on field trips.

Teachers can do something similar with an image of a student wrestler from a school in New Jersey having his hair cut in order to participate in a wrestling match in December 2019. After engaging students with the VTS questions, a teacher could transition to a research-based discussion about the disparate impact of school rules about hair on People of Color. Reading an article like Newsela's "New York City Just Banned Discrimination Based on Hair" can be a great springboard for exploring claim, reasoning, and evidence with students by having them ask the following questions:

- *What do I think?* (claim)
- *Why do I think this?* (reasoning)
- *How do I know this is the case?* (evidence)

You will find links to these pictures and articles in the online companion to this book.

# Breathe and Reflect

What images or photographs might you use with your students as you engage in VTS? ∎

_____

_____

_____

_____

_____

_____

_____

_____

_____

_____

_____

_____

_____

_____

_____

_____

_____

_____

_____

_____

_____

_____

_____

_____

_____

## FOUR CORNERS

The four corners strategy is another way teachers can support students to take a position, share the reasoning behind the position, and support that position with evidence. With this strategy, the teacher reads a statement about which students need to choose one of the following positions: Strongly Agree, Agree, Disagree, Strongly Disagree. The teacher can begin by sharing statements that students are likely to have strong opinions about. Here are some examples:

https://bit.ly/38eUoi1

- Gum should be banned from school.

- The voting age should be changed to sixteen.

- Students should be able to use their phones in school.

Once the statement is shared, students go to the corner of the room that aligns with their position. While in their corners, students discuss their perspective and rationale with the other students in the corner who share the same opinion. A representative from each group shares the group's reasoning for the position with the rest of the class.

You can then build on the experience by having students take a stand about more challenging topics and questions (e.g., Saying "All Lives Matter" or "Blue Lives Matter" is an appropriate response to "Black Lives Matter"), give the students the opportunity to discuss the rationale behind their opinions with their classmates, and begin to engage in research to find evidence to support their positions. If you're able, provide students with authentic audiences for their discourse sessions by inviting students from other classes to watch their discussions.

# Breathe and Reflect

Use this space to reflect on topics you think your students may want to explore using the four corners strategy. ■

_____

_____

_____

_____

_____

_____

_____

_____

_____

_____

_____

_____

_____

_____

_____

_____

_____

_____

_____

_____

_____

_____

_____

_____

_____

_____

_____

_____

_____

# INTEGRATING TECHNOLOGY INTO DISCOURSE

In addition to supporting student-centered learning by engaging students as active learners, providing the opportunity to differentiate instruction through individualized/small-group learning, and facilitating peer collaboration, integrating technology allows you to utilize online resources to support students as they explore debate topics and supports and to engage in critical thinking about complex issues.

- Create Debate (createdebate.com) is a social tool that democratizes the decision-making process through online debate.

- Debate.org is a free online community where people from around the world come to debate, read the opinions of others, and research today's most controversial topics and cast votes on opinion polls.

- Kialo Edu (https://www.kialo-edu.com) is a custom version of Kialo.com, the world's largest argument mapping and debate site specifically designed for classroom use. Its clear, visually compelling format makes it easy to follow the logical structure of a discussion and facilitates thoughtful collaboration. Kialo's mission is to promote well-reasoned discussion online, and to that end, Kialo is free for educators to use.

- *New York Times* Learning Network's Room for Debate (nytimes.com/roomfordebate) is a resource that invites knowledgeable outside contributors to discuss news events and other timely issues, and reader comments are moderated through the week.

- Pro/Con.org explores current issues from a nonpartisan perspective.

Providing students with the opportunity to learn how to research effectively, to understand the difference between fact and opinion by taking and defending a position based on evidence, and understanding multiple perspectives on complex issues are skills that will benefit students as learners and help them to develop into informed, inclusive, empathetic, equity-minded citizens who value truth and diverse contributions, perspectives, and experiences. In the next chapter, we will explore how to build on what students learn through discourse to seek solutions to complex societal issues through action-oriented learning.

# Breathe and Reflect

Use this space to reflect on technology resources you may want to use to support your students as they learn to engage in discourse. ∎

_____

_____

_____

_____

_____

_____

_____

_____

_____

_____

_____

_____

_____

_____

_____

_____

_____

_____

_____

_____

_____

_____

_____

_____

_____

_____

Now that we've spent time learning about ways to expand student access to and understanding of their racial identities, strategies for helping students to learn previously unknown content about perspectives other than White-centered views, and how to engage in challenging conversations, in Chapter 7 we'll focus on supporting students as they apply what they're discovering through action-oriented learning.

# Opening Windows Into Overlooked Challenges

## Action-Oriented Learning

On Day 2 of the The Equity Literacy Approach workshop in the fall of 2018, Paul Gorski asked us how we usually try to address the problem of homelessness. Several participants volunteered answers like "We run soup kitchens" and "We donate to coat drives." He then asked questions that have been sticking with me since that day. *Do any of these things actually address the problem of homelessness? What do those who are experiencing homelessness need most?* They need homes. The efforts we tend to support don't provide homes—they just attempt to make people experiencing homelessness a bit more comfortable while still not having a home. If we were to look at homelessness as an iceberg, coat drives and soup kitchens attempt to address what we see above the surface, but beneath the surface, the challenge is uninterrupted. When we apply this metaphor to antiracist teaching practices, we realize the importance of helping students discover the beneath-the-surface iceberg of the problem—systemic racism—and work toward finding solutions to that problem, in addition to solving more surface-level issues. This is where action-oriented learning can be invaluable if done with thoughtful, developmentally appropriate planning.

In Chapter 1, you read that James Banks believes that "to act" is one of the three goals of global citizenship education. As we are working with our students, it is important to keep in mind that the ultimate outcome of antibias, antiracist (ABAR) instructional practices is to inform and equip students to be change agents—to transition from awareness to action. This is where action-oriented learning comes in. Through action-oriented learning experiences, students can build on their growing awareness of societal challenges and begin to participate in solutions.

In order to learn how to solve complex problems, students will need to develop 21st century skills like planning, critical thinking, reasoning, communication, cross-cultural understanding, and decision-making. Action-oriented learning can help students to develop these skills by actively engaging in real-world and personally meaningful learning experiences.

This chapter will help teachers to integrate what students have learned about their own racial identity and the histories, perspectives, experiences, and lives of marginalized people to explore potential solutions to a related complex problem of their choosing. By incorporating effective ABAR practices, you will learn to help students effectively identify and address societal challenges.

Teachers have the opportunity to support students as they learn how to become change agents by taking responsibility and standing up against bullying, exclusion, prejudice, and injustice as well as speaking up when someone is wronged. This begins with noticing the things around us that are unfair and paying attention to how society can be better for everyone—starting with our school communities.

Students, even at a young age, can sense when something needs to change. In 2013, when Christian Bucks was a first grader at Roundtown Elementary School in Central York, Pennsylvania, he was inspired by a special bench he saw on the playground of a school in Germany. He shared his idea of creating a bench designed to help students experiencing loneliness during recess with his teacher and principal, and the following school year, the principal invited Christian to select a buddy bench for their schoolyard and to explain the purpose of the bench to the school board and school community. The story was initially picked up by a local newspaper, then a national newspaper, and then national media outlets. Students and school communities were inspired by this idea, and Christian helped to initiate a buddy bench movement across the country. (Interestingly, this occurred in Central York, Pennsylvania, where the school board attempted to ban a multitude of books and resources by and about People of Color. Student protests helped to alter that decision, just as Christian altered the experiences of students during recess.) Students have the power to be changemakers!

# Breathe and Reflect

Have you ever engaged in action-oriented learning as a student and/or as a teacher? Use this space to reflect on the experience, especially what compelled you to become involved. ■

_____

_____

_____

_____

_____

_____

_____

_____

_____

_____

_____

_____

_____

_____

_____

_____

_____

_____

_____

_____

_____

_____

_____

_____

_____

_____

# LAYING THE FOUNDATION FOR ACTION-ORIENTED LEARNING

You have probably heard the term *service learning*. I refer to these learning experiences as action-oriented learning for a couple of reasons. First, it's important to me to avoid the association with saviorism that can come with approaching work from a service mindset and for students to understand that they engage in this learning to transform their own thinking and ways of being by helping to meet the needs of others. Additionally, in order to continue the learning journey we've taken together so far in this book, building on the foundation of deepening understanding by taking action is essential. When I talk about action-oriented learning (which is sometimes referred to by practitioners as project-based learning, or PBL), it means to implement the five stages of design thinking to help students apply what they've learned about from exploring the histories, experiences, and perspectives of people who are racially different in order to become changemakers. Let's take a look at the stages through the lens of the challenge of homelessness cited at the beginning of this chapter:

- **Empathizing:** Helping students to connect with and understand the experiences of others without judgment (e.g., How does it feel to experience homelessness?).

- **Defining:** Supporting students to identify societal problems and needs (e.g., What is homelessness, and why do some people experience it? What do people experiencing homelessness need? Why are some people opposed to affordable housing in their communities?).

- **Ideating:** Students begin to explore potential solutions to challenges (e.g., How might we begin to help provide those experiencing homelessness with what they need?).

- **Prototyping:** Students create potential solutions to challenges (e.g., What if we start a campaign in our town to vote in favor of affordable housing in our community?).

- **Testing:** Students try out the solutions, solicit feedback, and refine the plan (e.g., How did voters respond to our affordable housing campaign? What do we need to do differently?).

Teachers support and facilitate learning by creating learning experiences for students that address the six criteria for high-quality PBL, including the following:

- **Intellectual challenge and accomplishment:** Ensure that students are thinking critically about a complex problem

- **Authenticity:** The learning experience needs to reflect what happens in the world outside of school

- **Public product:** Students share their work with the teacher, classmates, and people outside of school

- **Collaboration:** Contributing individual skills to a shared work with classmates and people beyond the school community

- **Project management:** Students learn how to manage time, tasks and resources effectively

- **Reflection:** Students reinforce and retain their learning by pausing throughout the process to assess their work, and consider how to make it better (High Quality Project Based Learning, n.d.)

You can use online tools like IDEO's "Design Thinking for Educators Co-Designing Schools Toolkit," and Edutopia's resources supporting PBL experiences. These resources are linked in the online companion to this book, found at resources.corwin.com/openwindows. Let's take a look at an example of how Shannon Hardy engaged in action-oriented learning with her students using design thinking.

## DESIGN THINKING: WORKING TO END RACISM

With the support of the Design for Change (DFC), an organization that empowers young innovators and activists to take on a project and change something for the better, Shannon Hardy, a National Board Certified eighth-grade teacher in Raleigh, North Carolina, leads her students through action-oriented learning based on the principles of design thinking. Through the design process, they are equipped to identify the problem, brainstorm, design, build, test, evaluate, redesign, and

https://bit.ly/3s7G6XZ

share solutions. Shannon begins, as all effective learning designers do, with an invitation for students to brainstorm what a perfect world would look like as a way to identify the challenges they'd like to address. Here's what Shannon's students said would reflect a perfect world for them:

- There would be equal treatment for everyone no matter your race, ethnicity, religion, sex, age, education, or sexual orientation.

- Governments would help the citizens of their country and other countries.

- People would admit to their country's mistakes in the past and give it their best effort to change what has been done.

- Everyone would have a place to sleep at night, clothes, food, and freedom.

- People would live their own lives without threats or the fear of being hurt, imprisoned, or killed.

- There would be no wars, and the world would be a world of peace.

If you were to support your students in an action-oriented learning experience, you can begin in the same way. Ask your students to share their version of a perfect world. They can begin working in pairs or small groups, then share out with the whole class to start shaping a class vision. How do you think your students would respond if you were to ask them to share their vision of a perfect world? Would their brainstorms reveal a desire for improvement to school experiences? Changes in their communities? Students' dreams of a perfect world could be as big as world peace and ending climate change or as seemingly small as a buddy bench or having the opportunity to meet more people who are racially, culturally, and/or ethnically different.

The narrative that can sometimes surround middle school students is that they are self-focused and don't spend much time serving others. This is not the case with Shannon's students, who worked to end racism during the 2017–2018 school year and continued into the 2018–2019 school year by sharing the story of Joe Holt Jr., who was the first Black student to challenge the segregated schools in Raleigh, North Carolina, in 1956 when he was thirteen; they also advocated for the removal of Confederate monuments in North Carolina. Shannon's students became changemakers not from a perspective of pity but of support and solidarity and provided an amazing example to their community.

In the sections that follow, I offer suggestions and resources you can use to replicate these projects, or use to model projects on topics your students choose.

## SCHOOL SEGREGATION, IN THE PAST AND PRESENT: THE JOE HOLT JR. STORY

Shannon's students learned about Joseph Holt, Jr., who, as previously mentioned, was the first Black student to challenge the segregated schools in Raleigh, North Carolina, in 1956 when he was thirteen when he applied to enroll in the all-White Josephus Daniels Junior High School, which was within walking distance from his house. Students had the opportunity to meet Mr. Holt and heard from him how separate was actually not equal because of the lack of equal education opportunities for Black students. One of the students in Shannon's class decided to write a biography about Joe Holt Jr. for his "Ending Racism"

https://bit.ly/36Cim6w

project, and one of his goals was for Joe Holt Jr. to receive a formal apology for what he and his family experienced.

Inspired by the learning experiences of his daughter and her classmates in Shannon's class, the parent of one of the students wrote a letter to the editor of a local newspaper on behalf of Joseph Holt, Jr., again asking the school board to remove the Daniels name from the middle school and name it, instead, for the Holt family. In the end, the school board did change the name (WRAL 2020). Unfortunately, they did not name it for the first Black family to seek a White seat after the *Brown v. Board* decision. Instead, they named the school after the Black community in which Joseph Holt, Jr. was raised—Oberlin Village (Leah 2020). When reflecting on the learning experiences of his daughter and her classmates in Shannon's class, he commented, "These kids, these times, are upending my whole attitude of resignation towards the world." When sharing this with me, Shannon stated, "This is why we must teach this way. We adults, parents included, are inspired by our youth's belief that justice is possible."

## What It Looks Like in Action

If you decide to engage your students in learning more about the historical impact of school segregation, one way to expand your students' awareness of school segregation issues could be to show and discuss a slideshow on the Ruby Bridges and the Civil Rights Movement: A Simple Act of Courage website (https://sn1.scholastic.com/issues/2018-19/020119.html). The website includes a slideshow for students in Grades K–2 and 3–8. Students can also learn more about the story of the Little Rock Nine using the "Little Rock Nine: Activities" resource, where students can read primary documents, watch and reflect on a short film, learn from art projects for self and community, and discover what's typically not included in social studies and history textbooks.

It would be helpful for students to understand that school segregation isn't just part of the history of the United States. It's a challenge we still face. Reading and discussing Newsela articles like "On the Anniversary of *Brown v. Board*, Evidence of Resegregation," where students can learn how Students of Color and students experiencing poverty are still isolated from their White peers and peers experiencing financial advantages, and "What School Segregation Looks Like in the U.S. Today in Four Charts," in which students can learn about the geographical differences in the racial composition of public schools in the United States as well as students' exposure to other racial groups. Newsela resources provide the opportunity to adjust the readability of the article to provide access to students reading at different levels. You can find these resources linked in the online companion to this book: resources.corwin.com/openwindows.

## Breathe and Reflect

Reflect on how you and your students have spoken up when someone has been hurt or wronged by bias. If this is not something you or your students have done yet, what can you do to lay the foundation for speaking up? ■

_____

_____

_____

_____

_____

_____

_____

_____

_____

_____

_____

_____

_____

_____

_____

_____

_____

_____

_____

_____

_____

_____

_____

_____

_____

_____

_____

## REMOVING CONFEDERATE MONUMENTS

Drum Majors for Justice (DM4J) is a youth service group formed by Shannon's former students dedicated to reconciling and resolving racial injustices in and around Wake County. The name comes from a quote from a sermon by Dr. Martin Luther King Jr. that states, "Yes, if you want to say that I was a Drum Major, say that I was a Drum Major for Justice. Say that I was a Drum Major for Peace. I was a Drum Major for Righteousness. And all of the other shallow things will not matter" (King 1968).

DM4J began as an elective at Exploris Middle School in downtown Raleigh and they have worked on several projects concerning racial injustice in the county. They continue to work closely with Mr. Joe Holt. Although he was unsuccessful, his experiences and story have allowed him to mentor students as they grow.

Going to school just two blocks away from the Confederate monuments at the Capitol building, students frequently passed by them on their way around the city. In light of the recent protests against racial hatred and White supremacy, they were inspired to #takehatedown so that North Carolina can finally move toward reconciliation. The Take Hate Down website and petition were developed by DM4J.

https://bit.ly/3v86tin

Their work also enabled them to apply to Design for Change (DFC). Their application gave them the ability to attend the first-ever DFC Children's Global Summit, which took place in Rome where they presented three of their projects alongside youth from all over the world.

Even though the Confederate statues are being removed from the Capitol, DM4J believes that there's still much more to do. They created a Change.org petition titled "We Demand You Repeal GS100-2.1 to Take Down the Confederate Monuments." G.S. 100-2.1 is the law that protects Confederate monuments and keeps them from being removed or placed in more suitable locations. If the law isn't repealed, the Confederate statues that were removed from the Capitol building will have to be returned. There are over 140 other monuments to the Confederacy around North Carolina that are still standing and can't be moved if this law doesn't change.

### What It Looks Like in Action

There's a connection between taking down Confederate monuments and changing the names of schools and teams with racist implications. If you choose to engage your students in learning about the impact of monuments and buildings named after White supremacists, and cultural misappropriation, you can check students' previous knowledge, clarify student understanding, share necessary background, and read and discuss the topic with the support of one or more of the following articles:

- "Teach This: Native American Appropriation at the Superbowl" | Learning for Justice

- "Set in Stone" | Learning for Justice

- "Panels Placed Near Confederate Statues Detail Their Racist History" | Newsela

- "'We Won't Wear the Name'" | Learning for Justice

To reflect on the process of changing a team's name, students can first read Newsela's "What's in a Name Change? The Logistics of Retiring and Creating a Team Name" and/or take a deep dive into the topic with Strategic Educational Research Partnership's WordGen Weekly unit, "Should the NFL Require the Washington Redskins to Change Their Name?" (1.19). Since the Washington team has changed its name, students can read Newsela's "Washington's NFL Team Drops its Nickname After 87 Years" and reflect on the considerations for and process of changing a team's name. These resources are all linked in the online companion to this book resources.corwin.com/openwindows.

# Breathe and Reflect

Reflect on a time when you became more aware of and developed empathy for a challenge that someone who identifies differently from you was facing, and you put your awareness of the challenge into action. This can be a time you may have been moved to sign a petition, donate to a cause, and/or volunteered for a community service project. What compelled you? What made you believe that your efforts would be effective? ▪

_____

_____

_____

_____

_____

_____

_____

_____

_____

_____

_____

_____

_____

_____

_____

_____

_____

_____

_____

_____

_____

_____

## REFLECTING ON THE FINAL PROJECT

Thinking back to what we learned earlier in the chapter about high-quality PBL, the sixth criteria is reflection. Reflection helps students to concretize, reinforce, assess, and retain what they have learned. Here are the questions that Shannon had her students engage with as they reflected on their "Ending Racism" final projects:

- Reflect on the past eight months. What emotions have you felt? When? Why? As we close, what emotions are you experiencing?

- Why did you want to join this [action-oriented] learning project?

- Did our actions develop empathy? How?

- What is the difference between charity and [action-oriented] learning? Did we stereotype at any time? How are we culturally sensitive? What assumptions did we make in an effort to be thoughtful?

- Who did we interview to help us develop empathy about racism? Who were the stakeholders? What did we learn?

- If we did nothing, what is the probable future?

- Are you catalysts for a tipping point that ends racism?

- Is designing change a clear path? What were the surprises?

- How has DFC changed you?

- What real-world skills do students learn?

- What's next? Should the "End Racism" [action-oriented] learning project continue?

Students in Shannon's classes used an emotions chart to identify whether they experienced happiness, fear, guilt, excitement, sorrow, jealousy, sadness, pride, tiredness, anger, boredom, love, embarrassment, surprise, shyness, and or/hope. Shannon then collected and shared the percentage of students who experienced each emotion. The primary emotions students identified were happy, proud, excited, empowered, and afraid.

Students chose this action-oriented learning project because they had seen or experienced racism themselves, or were shocked to learn about historical and current instances of racism, and wanted to do something to not only ensure that more people were aware of specific instances but to help end it as well. Having an impact on such a pervasive problem and working to try to repair harm was important to them.

Through action-oriented learning, students learn how sympathy and empathy differ. Sympathy tends to convey commiseration, pity, or feelings of sorrow for someone else who is experiencing misfortune, while empathy is the ability to imagine oneself in the situation of another, and developing an understanding of the emotions, ideas, or opinions of that person. This short film by Brené Brown explores the difference between sympathy and empathy in a memorable way.

https://bit.ly/3k4PpU4

Students also learn the difference between charity and action-oriented learning. Whereas charity is typically providing resources to a person, organization, or community one considers as being "in need," action-oriented learning is a strategy that integrates meaningful community service with instruction and reflection to enrich the learning experience, teach civic responsibility, and strengthen communities. In exploring the question of what the probable future would be if they did nothing, students realize that important stories might be forgotten, and there might be no reconciliation for people who were harmed.

Students in Shannon's classes shared that the action-oriented learning projects gave them opportunities to develop the following skills that will be formative for them as students and as citizens:

- Public speaking and using their voices to draw attention to and support for their project

- Interviewing and transcribing

- Writing e-mails to inquire

- Developing leadership skills

- Having increased confidence

- Discovering who you are

- Learning to see things from other perspectives

- Empathizing more

https://bit.ly/3xS6cSt

- Developing organizational skills

- Using tools like SignUpGenius to coordinate events and people

- Working under pressure

- Creating a GoFundMe crowdfunding campaign

- Telemarketing

- Learning how to load a truck

- Learning how to set an alarm clock

The action-oriented learning projects provided students with the opportunity to visualize and operationalize what they've learned about putting their diverse, equitable, and inclusive beliefs into action by learning about the world—including its perplexities and challenges and how to help make it better in practical ways. Though they encountered obstacles, it was helpful for them to learn how hard it can be to change people's minds and inequitable systems whether you're working toward changes that are big or small.

With the support of Malcolm Gladwell's (2002) *The Tipping Point: How Little Things Can Make a Big Difference*, students learned about the skills and resources they needed to become catalysts for a tipping point that moves us closer to ending racism and working for change. This is a learning experience that they wanted to continue, and have continued beyond middle school into high school.

When reflecting on her experiences facilitating these learning experiences with her students, Shannon shared, "At the end of each day the problem of racism is felt by every student, teacher, and parent. Exploring historic and current racism is authentic, relevant work that empowers our students to make our world better. My learning through this work with students, parents, and our community has made me a better human."

# Breathe and Reflect

Reflect on how you and your students can plan and carry out collective action against bias and injustice in the world. How will you evaluate what strategies are most effective (e.g., writing a letter to a newspaper or politician, starting a petition)? ■

_____

_____

_____

_____

_____

_____

_____

_____

_____

_____

_____

_____

_____

_____

_____

_____

_____

_____

_____

_____

_____

_____

_____

If you are unable to take your students to a museum focused on civil rights or antiracism, students can experience museums virtually. Take a look at the websites for the following museums for virtual options (links are also included in the online companion to this book):

- International Civil Rights Center & Museum

- National Museum of African American History and Culture

- National Museum of the American Indian

- National Museum of the American Latino (in development)

- National Museum of Asian Americans

- National Memorial for Peace and Justice

- Smithsonian Asian Pacific American Center

https://bit.ly/3OtX8c5

## INTERDISCIPLINARY CONNECTIONS

One of the benefits of action-oriented learning experiences for students is the opportunity to engage in interdisciplinary learning where students can build on their literacy skills and apply their growing awareness across content areas. You can explore real-life challenges with your students in a way that will equip them to build their awareness of and empathy for challenges that they and their families may not be familiar with.

Liz Caffrey (she/her) is a middle school math teacher at the Atrium School in Watertown, Massachusetts. Liz is passionate about math and math instruction and considers mathematics to be a dynamic, creative, and, most importantly, human endeavor. Liz believes that students deserve to see mathematics as relevant to their lives, but they should also experience the power, beauty, and elegance that is math. They should be taught how to use math as a lens to analyze, critique, and appreciate the world. Using important articles about current events and statistics every week creates an experience for her students that pushes them to analyze and question real-world data. Projects encourage students to see connections between math and other subjects as well as to have fun while applying their math skills in ways they never thought possible. And when they reflect back, they see themselves as doers and creators of new mathematics—as mathematicians.

Liz explores income gaps, redlining, and financial literacy with her eighth-grade students through the Life on a Budget Project. The challenge in the Life on a Budget Project is for students to take on the role of a financial adviser and create a monthly budget spreadsheet for a new client, including a one-page written summary of spending recommendations.

Through this project, students learn about the history and causes of wealth inequality in the United States, including an exploration of wealth distribution as well as a case study about a redlining incident in 2015. They research and reflect on how race, gender, and education impact economic mobility in the United States and abroad by exploring the following discussion questions:

- Look at the redlining data for your town and two other cities and towns. What do you notice?

- What injustices does the census data reveal? What did the articles illuminate in terms of causes for these injustices?

- How might the statistics we have seen be misused to create stereotypes about the capabilities of different racial and gender demographics?

- If you were to fund a nonprofit to help address the issue of income inequality, where would you start? What would your cause be, and how would you fight for more equality? What would be some ways you could narrow the wage gap?

Students are then assigned a client for whom the student files the taxes, finds an apartment, creates a monthly budget, and writes up budget recommendations. To do this effectively, students must research the cost of living in Massachusetts, where the school is located, as well as federal and state tax, social security, and Medicare withholdings.

Clients are broken down by race, (binary) gender, and education level based on US census data (e.g., the mean earnings of a Black female with a doctorate in 2018 was $94,134, and for a White male it was $146,076), and students are asked to state what they notice and wonder about the data. To complete the project effectively, students must do as follows:

- Build on the knowledge gained as depicted in the Life on a Budget student spreadsheet, which contains federal tax bracket information, withholdings, monthly and yearly net and gross salary considerations as well as living expenses like food, clothing, health insurance, rent, utilities, phone, Internet, car loans (or public transit costs), car insurance and maintenance, and savings.

- Build on the knowledge gained when learning about what life really looks like on a budget by playing the role of a budget planner, taking a person's financial resources into consideration.

- Reflect on what content-based knowledge, practical life lessons, and social justice knowledge they gained by engaging in this project.

# Breathe and Reflect

Use this space to reflect on ways you have engaged students in interdisciplinary learning and what you notice and wonder about Liz Caffrey's Life on a Budget Project. ■

_____

_____

_____

_____

_____

_____

_____

_____

_____

_____

_____

_____

_____

_____

_____

_____

_____

_____

_____

_____

_____

_____

_____

_____

_____

_____

_____

_____

_____

At the conclusion of an action-oriented learning opportunity, you can support your students to reflect on what they learned as they engaged with the project and to determine next steps. In order to be compelled into action, students must learn to empathize with someone or a group who is experiencing a challenge. It can be a challenge they're familiar with and also something they learn to understand by connecting with people who are experiencing the challenge. The best way to concretize their learning is to apply it by taking informed action—not from a place of pity but from a place of solidarity with others in the human family. The decision to act is not an easy one, and sometimes involves risk, but with effective preparation, and practice, and a community working together toward the same purpose, it is possible to become a change agent in this world.

# Epilogue
## Find Your Marigolds

In these pages we have taken an important journey together. We've explored our own racial identity development and learned how to support students as they develop an awareness of the same. We have prepared to navigate resistance and engage in critical conversations. We have learned ways to support students as they discover unknown histories, contributions, experiences, and perspectives and also how to engage our students with authentic, action-oriented learning experiences.

We began with the frame of helping students to experience more windows. As we conclude our journey together, let's reflect on what it takes to engage in and sustain this hard but good work. What we must always keep in mind is that students can do hard things when given the opportunity and skills to do so. I loved my elementary school and my teachers, especially in fourth and fifth grade. I looped with the same two teachers for those grades, and I remember reading Shakespeare with and learning Latin from those teachers. And it wasn't little kid versions of Shakespeare. We read the actual texts of *Hamlet, Macbeth, Julius Caesar, Romeo and Juliet,* and *A Midsummer Night's Dream.* Although I appreciated learning what felt like advanced content as an eight- or nine-year-old, the content was Eurocentric. If they were able to engage us at that age with that content, then teachers can absolutely engage students with antibias, antiracist (ABAR) instructional practices. The key question is, are we willing?

It's important to have the space to know that we are going to be messy, because as with anything, despite our best intentions, we're going to make mistakes and sometimes say or do the wrong thing. The only way to the other side of where we find ourselves now is through the hard parts. When you're learning anything, whether it be playing an instrument, speaking another language, or performing a dance routine, you will make mistakes as you learn. All the things that we learn how to do start out a bit wobbly. When we're learning how to ride a bike, we probably fell . . . a lot! It's like that in the beginning, and as you practice and refine your approach, you fall less. The falls won't be as plentiful as they are in the beginning. But we have to be able to apply that same growth mindset to this work. It's going to start

https://bit.ly/3k2bS3V

out messy, but we'll get better at it the more we do it. We shouldn't let the desire to be perfect get in the way of our progress.

Shannon Pitcher-Boyea (she/her/hers), the director of Instructional Support Services for Grades 3–4 with the Franklin-Essex-Hamilton Boards of Cooperative Educational Services (FEH BOCES), shared with me the concept of *finding your marigolds* explored in Jennifer Gonzalez's (2013) article, *Find Your Marigold: The One Essential Rule for New Teachers*. Shannon explains, "So marigolds, if you put them around a garden, they protect your garden from harm. Find your marigolds means find your people—the people who will guard you. You can't do this work by yourself. And if you haven't found them, keep looking because they're there. You'll know who they are. You need a network where you can support one another."

As a part of the research for this book, I interviewed ABAR practitioners around the country—elementary, middle, and high school teachers as well as staff developers, consultants, State Teachers of the Year from urban, suburban, and rural school districts. In the online companion to this book, you can learn from those who have tools to share with us for our journeys within our own school communities. These educators are marigolds for me, and I hope that they will be the same for you.

Rudine Sims Bishop (1990) states, when reflecting on the concept of windows and mirrors, "When lighting conditions are just right . . . a window can also be a mirror. Literature transforms human experience and reflects it back to us, and in that reflection we can see our own lives and experiences as part of the larger human experience." I mentioned at the beginning of the book what my hopes are for you and your students, dear reader. May you open the minds of your students by opening windows for and with them, and may those open windows be bathed in the light of truth, thereby creating a mirror that reflects back to us all who we were truly meant to be.

Love always,

Afrika (aka, Your Marigold)

# References

Adichie, Chimamanda Ngozi. 2009. "The Danger of a Single Story." Filmed 2009. TEDGlobal video, 18:33. https://www.ted.com/talks/chimamanda_ngozi_adichie_the_danger_of_a_single_story?language=en.

Aguilar, Elena. 2018. *Onward: Cultivating Emotional Intelligence in Educators*. San Francisco: Jossey-Bass.

Ahiyya, Vera. 2022. *Rebellious Read Alouds*. Thousand Oaks, CA: Sage.

American Debate League. 2022. "Benefits of Debate." https://www.americandebateleague.org/benefits-of-debate.html.

Baldwin, James. 1962. "As Much Truth as One Can Bear; to Speak Out About the World as It Is, Says James Baldwin, Is the Writer's Job as Much of the Truth as One Can Bear." *New York Times*, January 14, 1962, BR11.

Baldwin, James. (1963) n.d. "A Talk to Teachers." *Saturday Review*, December 21, 1963. Reprint, Zinn Education Project. https://www.zinnedproject.org/materials/baldwin-talk-to-teachers.

Banks, James. 2007. *Educating Citizens in a Multicultural Society*. 2nd ed. New York: Teachers College Press.

Bishop, Rudine Sims. 1990. "Mirrors, Windows, and Sliding Glass Doors." *Perspectives: Choosing and Using Books for the Classroom* 6(3): ix–xi.

Borysenko, Karlyn (@DrKarlynB). 2022. "Tomorrow, we start building an army of parents armed with the skills to torture woke teachers and administrators in schools with mountains of public records requests. Let's find out what they're really teaching. Learn how in this free event: activelyunwoke.com/events/." Twitter, February 10, 2022, 12:02 p.m. https://twitter.com/DrKarlynB/status/1491834866110980102.

Carson, Jo. 1993. *Stories I Ain't Told Nobody Yet*. New York: Theater Communications Group.

Children's Community School. 2018. "They're Not Too Young to Talk About Race." http://www.childrenscommunityschool.org/social-justice-resources/.

Cisneros, Sandra. 1991. "My Name." In *The House on Mango Street*. New York: Vintage Books.

Coates, Ta-Nehisi. 2015. *Between the World and Me*. New York: Spiegel and Grau.

Dahlen, Sarah Park. 2019. "Picture This: Diversity in Children's Books 2018 Infographic." June 19, 2019. https://readingspark.wordpress.com/2019/06/19/picture-this-diversity-in-childrens-books-2018-infographic/.

Dawsey, Josh, and Felicia Sonmez. 2022. "'Legitimate Political Discourse': Three Words About Jan. 6 Spark Rift Among Republicans." *Washington Post*, February 8, 2022. https://www.washingtonpost.com/politics/2022/02/08/gop-legitimate-political-discourse/.

Denevi, Elizabeth, and Lori Cohen. 2020. "White Antiracist Activists." Teaching While White. https://www.teachingwhilewhite.org/resources/white-antiracist-activists.

Dunham, Yarrow, Andrew S. Baron, and Mahzarin R. Banaji. 2008. *The Development of Implicit Intergroup Cognition. Trends in Cognitive Sciences* 12(7): 248–253.

EdWeek Research Center. 2020. "Anti-Racist Teaching: What Educators Really Think." *EdWeek.* September 25, 2020. https://www.edweek.org/leadership/anti-racist-teaching-what-educators-really-think/2020/09.

Gibran, Kahlil. n.d. 1883–1931. "On Children." https://poets.org/poem/children-1?mbd=1.

Gill, Jeff. 2013. "Trooper, Photographer Reflect on Iconic Photo." *Gainesville Times,* January 22, 2013. https://www.gainesvilletimes.com/news/trooper-photographer-reflect-on-iconic-photo/.

Gladwell, Malcolm. 2002. *The Tipping Point: How Little Things Can Make a Big Difference.* New York: Back Bay Books.

Gonzalez, Jennifer. 2013. "Find Your Marigold: The One Essential Rule for New Teachers." Cult of Pedagogy. August 29, 2013. https://www.cultofpedagogy.com/marigolds/.

Helms, Ann. 2015. "Bree Newsome, James Tyson Talk About SC Confederate Flag Grab." *Charlotte Observer,* July 7, 2015. https://www.charlotteobserver.com/news/local/article26578984.html.

Helms, J. E. (2008). *A Race Is a Nice Thing to Have: A Guide to Being a White Person or Understanding the White Persons in Your Life.* 2nd ed. Hanover, MA: Microtraining Associates.

High Quality Project Based Learning. n.d. *A Framework for High Quality Project Based Learning.* https://hqpbl.org/.

Hill, Daniel. (2020). *White Lies: Nine Ways to Expose and Resist the Racist Systems That Divide Us.* Grand Rapids, MI: Zondervan.

Holland, Kimberly. 2021. "Amygdala Hijack: When Emotion Takes Over." Healthline. https://www.healthline.com/health/stress/amygdala-hijack.

King, Martin Luther, Jr. 1968. "The Drum Major Instinct." Stanford: The Martin Luther King, Jr. Research and Education Institute. https://kinginstitute.stanford.edu/encyclopedia/drum-major-instinct.

King, Ruth. 2018. *Mindful of Race: Transforming Racism from the Inside Out.* Boulder, CO: Sounds True, Inc.

Kleinrock, Liz. 2021. *Start Here, Start Now: A Guide to Antibias and Antiracist Work in Your School Community.* Portsmouth, NH: Heinemann.

Ladd, Donna. 2011. "Fannie Lou Hamer." https://www.jacksonfreepress.com/news/2011/apr/15/fannie-lou-hamer/.

Leah, Heather. 2020. "Oberlin Village: A Community Built By People Freed From Slavery in Raleigh." WRAL. https://www.wral.com/oberlin-village-a-community-built-by-people-freed-from-slavery-in-raleigh/19148522/.

Learning for Justice. n.d. *Let's Talk!: Facilitating Critical Conversations With Students.* https://www.learningforjustice.org/magazine/publications/lets-talk.

Lester, Neil. "For White Allies in Search of a Solution to Racism/When Folks of Color Are Exhausted." Learning for Justice, August 29, 2017, https://www.learningforjustice.org/magazine/for-white-allies-in-search-of-a-solution-to-american-racism-when-folks-of-color-are.

Love, Bettina L. 2019. *We Want to Do More Than Survive: Abolitionist Teaching and the Pursuit of Educational Freedom.* Boston: Beacon Press.

Love, Bettina, and Chelsey Culley-Love (hosts). 2021, January 28. "Anneliese Singh: Author of the Racial Healing Handbook" (audio podcast episode). In *Teaching to Thrive.* Abolitionist Teaching Network. https://podcasts.apple.com/us/podcast/anneliese-singh-author-of-the-racial-healing-handbook/id1525043025?i=1000506928784.

Lyons, George Ella. 1993. *Where I'm From.* http://www.georgeellalyon.com/where.html.

Mayer, Henry. 1998. *All on Fire: William Lloyd Garrison and the Abolition of Slavery.* New York: St. Martin's Press, 118–120.

McGhee, Heather. 2021. *The Sum of Us.* New York: Random House.

Menakem, Resmaa. 2014. "White Supremacy as a Trauma Response." *Medium.* https://medium.com/@rmenakem/white-supremacy-as-a-trauma-response-ce631b82b975.

Menakem, Resmaa. 2017. *My Grandmother's Hands: Racialized Trauma and the Pathway to Mending Our Hearts and Bodies.* Las Vegas, NV: Central Recovery Press.

Mulholland, Loki (director). 2013. *An Ordinary Hero: The True Story of Joan Trumpauer Mulholland.* Taylor Street Films.

Mulholland, Loki. 2016. *She Stood for Freedom: The Untold Story of a Civil Rights Hero, Joan Trumpauer Mulholland.* Salt Lake City, UT: Shadow Mountain Publishing.

Okun, Tema. n.d. "White Supremacy Culture Characteristics: The Characteristics of White Supremacy Culture." *DRWorksBook.* https://www.dismantlingracism.or/white-supremacy-culture.html.

Parents League of New York. 2020. "Understanding Racial Identity: An Interview with Beverly Daniel Tatum." *Parents League of New York*, June 4, 2020. https://www.parentsleague.org/blog/understanding-racial-identity-interview-beverly-daniel-tatum.

Paterson, Katherine. 1978. *The Great Gilly Hopkins.* New York: T. Y. Crowell.

Payne, Ruby. 2005. *A Framework for Understanding Poverty.* 4th rev. ed. Highlands, TX: aha! Process, Inc.

Payne, Ruby. 2018. *A Framework for Understanding Poverty.* 6th ed. Highlands, TX: aha! Process, Inc.

Pranikoff, Kara. 2017. *Teaching Talk: A Practical Guide to Fostering Student Thinking and Conversation.* Portsmouth, NH: Heinemann.

Rosati, Juliana. 2020. "Recasting the Moment: Professor Howard Stevenson on Creating Change Through Racial Literacy." Penn GSE. October 22, 2020. https://www.gse.upenn.edu/news/recasting-moment-professor-howard-stevenson-creating-change-through-racial-literacy.

Saad, Layla F. 2020. *Me and White Supremacy: Combat Racism, Change the World, and Become a Good Ancestor.* Naperville, IL: Sourcebooks.

Simmons, Aija. 2019. "Using VTS to Teach Claim, Evidence, Reasoning, and Writing." VTS. April 10, 2019. https://vtshome.org/2019/04/10/using-vts-to-teach-claims-evidence-reasoning-and-writing/.

Singh, Anneliese. 2019. *The Racial Healing Handbook.* Oakland, CA: New Harbinger Publications.

Smith, Clint. 2014. "The Danger of Silence." Filmed July 2014. TED video, 4:10. https://www.ted.com/talks/clint_smith_the_danger_of_silence?referrer=playlist-10_great_talks_to_celebrate_bl.

Smith, Clint. 2016. *Counting Descent.* Portland, OR: Write Bloody Publishing.

Smith, Clint. 2021. *How the Word Is Passed: A Reckoning With the History of Slavery Across America.* New York: Little, Brown and Company.

Stevenson, Howard. 2017. "How to Resolve Racially Stressful Situations." Filmed October 2017. TED video, 17:26. https://www.ted.com/talks/howard_c_stevenson_how_to_resolve_racially_stressful_situations?language=en.

Style, Emily. 1988. "Curriculum as Window and Mirror." The National SEED Project. https://nationalseedproject.org/Key-SEED-Texts/curriculum-as-window-and-mirror.

Tatum, Beverly Tatum. 2017a. "Is My Skin Brown Because I Drank Chocolate Milk?" Filmed 2017. TEDxStanford video, 13:24. https://tedx.stanford.edu/lineup/beverly-daniel-tatum.

Tatum, Beverly Tatum. 2017b. *"Why Are All the Black Kids Sitting Together in the Cafeteria?": And Other Conversations About Race.* New York: Basic Books.

Thempra Social Pedagogy. n.d. "The Learning Zone Model." http://www.thempra.org.uk/social-pedagogy/key-concepts-in-social-pedagogy/the-learning-zone-model/.

Tutu, Desmond. 1984. "Nobel Lecture." https://www.nobelprize.org/prizes/peace/1984/tutu/lecture/.

Varela, Keosha. 2016. "Death Row Attorney Bryan Stevenson on 4 Ways to Fight Against Injustice." Aspen Institute. July 20, 2016. https://www.aspeninstitute.org/blog-posts/death-row-attorney-bryan-stevenson-4-ways-fight-injustice/.

Watson, Lilla. n.d. Lilla International Women's Network. https://lillanetwork.wordpress.com/about/.

Wiles, Deborah. 2005. *Freedom Summer.* New York: Aladdin Paperbacks.

WRAL. 2020. "Wake County School Board Moves Quickly to Change Name of School." https://www.wral.com/wake-county-school-board-moves-quickly-to-change-name-of-school/19147680/.

# Index

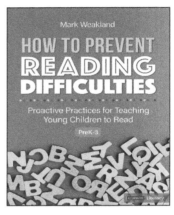
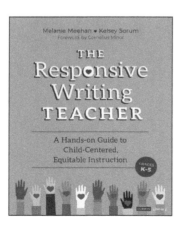

At Corwin Literacy we have put together a collection of just-in-time, classroom-tested, practical resources from trusted experts that allow you to quickly find the information you need when you need it.

**DOUGLAS FISHER, NANCY FREY, NICOLE LAW**

Using a structured, three-pronged approach—skill, will, and thrill—students experience reading as a purposeful act with this new comprehensive model of reading instruction.

**PAM KOUTRAKOS**

Packed with ready-to-go lessons and tools, this user-friendly resource provides ways to weave together different aspects of literacy using one mentor text.

**REBECCA G. HARPER**

Customizable strategies turn students' informal writing into a springboard for daily writing practice in every content area—with a focus on academic vocabulary, summarizing, and using textual evidence.

**MELANIE MEEHAN, CHRISTINA NOSEK, MATTHEW JOHNSON, DAVE STUART JR., MATTHEW R. KAY**

This series offers actionable answers to your most pressing questions about teaching reading, writing, and ELA.

CLN21BS0

**A SAGE Publishing Company**

**CORWIN HAS ONE MISSION:** to enhance education through intentional professional learning.

We build long-term relationships with our authors, educators, clients, and associations who partner with us to develop and continuously improve the best evidence-based practices that establish and support lifelong learning.